America in Therapy

PRAISE FOR *AMERICA IN THERAPY*

America in Therapy is powerful, clear, hopeful, and courageous—a perfect blend of stories, narration, and research, both honest about the severity of our problems and hopeful about our ability to heal.

—**Charlotte Taft**, MA Social Psychologist

Phyllis's unique ability to take real-life situations and give answers and hope to things I had never considered lit up my life with hope that it is possible to truly heal ourselves. I am forever changed and grateful to Phyllis for the courage and love it took to write *America in Therapy*. The whole world needs these extraordinary answers to the dilemma we are in so we can create a loving world for everyone.

—**Karin Grumstrup**, RN, NP, Poet

Phyllis is brilliant! She genuinely cares about making the world a better place. *America in Therapy* is going to impact the world in a very profound way.

—**Desiree Maya**, Professional Certified Coach (PCC), Author and Host of *The Born Unbreakable* Podcast

I was blown away by Phyllis Leavitt's knowledge and expertise regarding today's social and political climate. Our conversation echoed what has been on my mind for quite some time, yet she was able to articulate it better than I ever could. I highly recommend *America in Therapy* and having Phyllis Leavitt as a speaker if you're looking for an insightful and thought-provoking conversation.

—**Kendrick Grey**, Host of *The Dredloc Blerd* Podcast and up and coming Actor and Action Star

It is rare to find someone who is keenly knowledgeable, highly intuitive, as well as deeply compassionate for others. Phyllis is all three. *America in Therapy* is powerful and inspiring. It is an honor to read her and know her.

—**Dr. Heather Browne**, PsyD, LMFT, Author

AMERICA
IN
THERAPY

A NEW APPROACH TO
Hope and Healing for a Nation in Crisis

PHYLLIS E. LEAVITT, MA

NEW YORK

LONDON • NASHVILLE • MELBOURNE • VANCOUVER

America in Therapy

A New Approach to Hope and Healing for a Nation in Crisis

Published in New York, New York, by Morgan James Publishing. Morgan James is a trademark of Morgan James, LLC. www.MorganJamesPublishing.com

Proudly distributed by Publishers Group West®

ISBN 9781636983363 paperback
ISBN 9781636983370 ebook
Library of Congress Control Number: 2023946922

Cover Design by:
Chris Treccani
www.3dogcreative.net

Interior Design by:
Christopher Kirk
www.GFSstudio.com

Morgan James is a proud partner of Habitat for Humanity Peninsula and Greater Williamsburg. Partners in building since 2006.

Get involved today! Visit: www.morgan-james-publishing.com/giving-back

DEDICATION

*This book is dedicated to all of us—to those who know we have the
opportunity to create for our children and all future generations a safe,
peaceful, and loving world—and to those who do not yet know.*

TABLE OF CONTENTS

ACKNOWLEDGMENTS

I would like to thank my husband, Richard Jenkins, for his unwavering love and support for me to write this book and his belief in my message; my daughter, Isabella Braveheart, for being a source of profound inspiration through her own creative work and for pushing me to always take the next risk, jump off the next cliff; my two sons, Eddie and Daniel Konold, for their loving support and belief in me and my work; and my dear friends and writing companions Charlotte Taft and Anne Lewis, who have given me invaluable feedback and unwavering affirmation of the value of *America in Therapy*. I also want to thank Taryn Weiland for her expert editing of my book. She gave even more order and clarity to the complexity of all I wanted to express.

I need a separate paragraph to thank Ashley Mansour, my number one writing coach, mentor, and priceless guide through the entire writing process. Ashley saw beyond my own vision for the book from our very first meeting. Her brilliant assessment of my goals for *America in Therapy* and her coaching and editing expertise can never be fully acknowledged, but I will just say thank you, Ashley, with all my heart.

And a huge declaration of gratitude to Morgan James Publishing for accepting my manuscript and partnering with me to bring *America in Therapy* to all those who are ready and eager for this message.

Dear Reader,

I want to prepare you to learn something new and especially to be challenged to re-think all your beliefs about good guys and the bad guys. Be ready to discard some of the most treasured scripts we humans have been writing and reenacting for thousands of years that inevitably culminate in war between good and evil. And most of all, be ready to be inspired to play a new part in this play for the sake of the ultimate survival, not only of America but of humanity.

These are big ideas, and, in fact, we are at a very precarious time in human history that calls for big ideas and even bigger solutions. While we have evolved to a place of incredible brilliance and mastery and have produced countless mind-boggling technologies, we have simultaneously developed the means to obliterate ourselves and life as we know it. This terrifying paradox that our most creative and destructive abilities are now inextricable can be understood as the ultimate climax in the human drama. Many people are waking up to the urgency to rewrite the script before it is too late . . . and many are not. *America in Therapy* is dedicated to uncovering the little-known secrets of how we got ourselves out on this ledge, what keeps us here, and what is needed to restore us to safety.

The little-known secrets I will share with you come straight out of many years of experience as a psychotherapist and as a client myself. They are not actually secrets. The answers we need are lying hidden in plain sight. Hidden because the very things that have put us in such danger are the same things that keep us from recognizing it, sounding the alarm, and taking action to protect and save ourselves.

You see, dear reader, it is not our differing ideologies or even our most lethal weapons that have put us at such great risk, serious as these threats are. It is our deteriorating mental health that poses the greatest threat to our continued survival. Why? Because it is a terribly disturbed psychological state that condones the creation of weapons of mass destruction and justifies unleashing them on thousands upon thousands of innocent people. This is the greatest threat to our continued existence. I hope, dear reader, you will give yourself a moment to take this in.

But all is not lost. There is unquestionably cause for hope. Just as the best medical diagnosis offers the greatest hope for healing our bodies, the best psychological diagnosis offers the greatest hope for healing our wounded hearts, distorted thinking, and most destructive behaviors.

In the field of psychology, we now understand many of the causes of hatred and violence, which makes us better able to help victims heal and prevent the cycle of abuse from repeating.

Hope lies in the fact that the same tools we use to heal ourselves and our families of dysfunction, abuse, and neglect—these same tools can be used to heal a community, a state, *and a nation.*

There is unquestionably cause for hope that we can steer ourselves in the direction of our own rescue and sustainability if we commit to using what we already know works for the sake of the common good. It may take everything we have to make this 180-degree shift, but there is hope if we allow ourselves to look and act with a new psychological lens on our conditioning, our behavior, and on all that we know can restore us to safety. In *America in Therapy*, I give you, dear reader, my take on what that new lens is.

The only revolution we should be funding is a psychological re-evolution.

Chapter 1:

A WORLD ON THE BRINK

had a waking dream that America came to me for therapy. She looked like the Statue of Liberty, but her torch was cracked, and the flame had gone out.

This isn't working, she said as she tried to adjust her falling crown. *There is so much pain, hostility, and violence in our country. Why can't we sit down together and make a world for our children that is safe and green and welcoming for everyone?* She carefully arranged her robes around herself as if preparing for a long journey. Then she looked bravely into my eyes, a mixture of fear and hope on her face.

Let's talk, I told her. She was ready. She placed her stone tablet in her lap, lowered her torch to her side, and dove in.

She told me that we have huge gaps between the rich and the poor that are not being filled. Children were taken from their parents and put in cages. Minorities are openly targeted, and hate crimes and mass murders are accelerating with frightening speed. Our Capitol was invaded, and we are so polarized that some are talking about civil war. And if that weren't enough, as a country and a planet, we are hovering on the brink of our own extinction, with our stockpile of nuclear weapons and the continued destruction of the environment we depend on. *There are so many kind and generous people in America*, she said, *yet the rally cries for peaceful solutions are being drowned out, and so often now, those who march for peace and brotherly love are being assaulted, teargassed, and jailed.*

You don't need to wonder why my torch is not lit, she finally finished, her crown drooping on her forehead.

I know, I say. *And I cannot tell you how happy I am that you're here talking to me today. I have questioned along with you why there is not an overwhelming call to heal the enormous suffering we inflict on so many of our own people and in countries across the globe. I'm afraid we are a nation in denial of how much we are a danger to ourselves.*

As a psychotherapist, my job is to help bring peace to suffering people of all ages. My job is to help restore love and connection for those whose relationships are broken and injurious, whose children are lost and hurting, and many of whom have, themselves, endured pain and violation from others that they have never received any help to recover from. We still seem to live in an us-and-them mentality. We're still being fed and feeding ourselves the absurd belief that certain people are intrinsically evil, unworthy, and undeserving and that we need bigger, more lethal weapons to survive when we know they would devastate the planet and billions of us would die. Yet, the peace and love marches of the sixties seem to be long over. Whatever the spark was that shone so brightly then and that people of my generation thought surely would pave the way for a new world somehow went out or was lost in the shuffle to get ahead, put the World Wars behind us, make our fortunes, and focus on the latest and greatest technologies. Many people feel powerless to change courses before we either destroy the planet or lose all sense of our shared humanity, care, and compassion for one another.

Yes, America says, *It was the desire to offer a safe haven that kept my flame burning. Now, we not only don't offer it, but we ourselves are not safe here. The rising tide of violence and extremism is loud, angry, and threatening. Peaceful people are not. Is that part of the problem?* America asks. *Is there not a way for a peace initiative to be a powerful rally cry, a real force to be reckoned with?*

That is my goal, I say—a rally cry for peace. Like you, I tell America, *I want to understand why, with such amazing intelligence, creativity, technological know-how, and spirit of exploration, adventure, and innovation, we are not desperate to invest in the art and science of human relations when it is our failed human relations that now put us at such great risk. This is what I want to explore with you in depth,* I tell America.

What we have learned from the field of psychology helps us create optimal conditions for our well-being and future functioning in the world around us. In a nutshell, as a psychotherapist, I seek to understand why, with all the horrors of World War II in particular, we have not figured out that our most urgent investment should be in *how to get along with each other.* Partisanship has drowned out partnership, and it is tearing us apart from the inside out. The New York Times recently reported as the 2022 midterm elections approached that individual families all over America were now torn apart by politics. The article cited one family was made up of a Republican, a Libertarian, and two Democrats. One of them moved into a hotel to weather the elections by herself because of the extreme divisiveness at home. Another family member said, "I do consider . . . the political atmosphere in the house to be the biggest contributor to my mental health problems." The Times went on to say that this story is now ordinary in America, that in many families, the subject of politics has strained marriages and divided parents and children, and that since Donald Trump left office, politics are increasingly fueled by misinformation and hostile partisanship, which have pushed families to the breaking point. And yet, our families are the foundation of life for most of us. The emotional and mental conditions we are raised in have everything to do with our well-being and our future functioning in the world.[1]

I don't believe these great divisions between us are really the truth of who we are or who we want to be. As a psychotherapist, I have a completely different lens on conflict and the ways people become alienated from one another. The whole field of psychology and psychotherapy is designed to address and *heal the wars we are waging in our personal lives*—the ongoing internal battles we have with ourselves and all the wars, large and small, with our partners, children, friends, those we work with, and others in our immediate circles.

This is the key! I tell America. *Psychology today is an oasis in the desert that we have been ignoring as if we don't see the trees right in front of us.*

The whole field of psychology is designed to *restore* us to peace, love, and cooperation and help us develop the tools we need to return to safety and connection when we disagree. People come to therapy because they are aching to get out of the conflicts and stuck places in their lives and, most often, in their relationships as well. My rally cry is that we allow ourselves to feel the pain of all the wars we are in at home and around the world and come to therapy as a nation and afford ourselves of all the benefits psychology has to offer us—before it is too late!

Psychology is not an exact science. We are complicated beings with countless variables that contribute to our feelings, beliefs, and behaviors in any given moment. There is no one-size-fits-all answer to any question about why we humans do what we do, but the best psychotherapy helps us uncover the causes of our pain and dysfunction, heal from its worst effects, and opens the possibility of new ways of being that are more relational and life-giving. *And* it teaches us how to come back to connection when we are triggered into old self-sabotaging behaviors and power struggles. It is highly unlikely that conflict will disappear. It is as much in the nature of human beings to disagree, get angry, and want to dominate as it is that we long to come together, feel love and belonging, and cooperate for our mutual welfare. Psychology offers the skills and the hope for us to come back together before more serious harm is done.

In all my years of being a psychotherapist, there is not one healing technique I have ever learned that advocates *more* hatred and violence as a solution to our personal problems. And I have never met one person who wanted more conflict, more disconnection, and hatred in their lives. There is not a single person I have worked with or know, for that matter, who does not want more love, belonging, and peace. *We suffer in proportion to the ways love and all its beautiful side effects have been missing, lost, betrayed, and violated by other people.* Yet, as a nation, we have not even factored love and connection into our political agenda!

An Alarming Gap in Priorities

There is an enormous gap between what we want and value for ourselves and our loved ones—peace, love, adequate resources, safety, and cooperation—and the vicious wars on our own citizens we condone, to say nothing of the wars we fund and wage around the world. The assault we witness on minorities would be devastating if it were turned on us. The abandonment and exploitation of the poor we allow and tolerate if enough of us—and especially those in power—are well-fed might be considered a case for Social Services or deemed criminal if we were to impose it on our own children.

This gap is *a sign of psychological ill health.* Not practicing with others what we want for ourselves is a psychological issue. We have been led to believe that excessive use of force, the targeting of certain populations, and assault on the personal rights of "others," to name just a few of the terrors we face, are due to ideological or political differences when in fact *they are signs of mass mental illness that have infused politics and ideology.* We have been led to believe that neglect of whole segments of our population, verbal and physical violence, and the threats of violence that now inflame our differences are caused by opposing political affiliations and ideologies, but in fact, they are symptoms of a terribly disturbed mental state—what I call mass mental illness.

In our own homes, hopefully, we know better. We know that violence is abuse. Neglect is abuse. Yet we are living in a culture that tolerates and promotes abuse and neglect of others, and it is causing us to be mentally disturbed. Emotionally and mentally healthy people don't withhold the necessities of life from others or verbally assault them, nor do they urge others to do so. They do not exploit others or target them based on their beliefs, gender, race, or religion. Yes, mentally healthy people also become angry and fearful or strenuously disagree, but they restrain themselves from hurting other people. They do their best to work things out when they stray, come back to the table, are accountable for their behavior, make amends, and try again.

Psychology Holds Answers

Psychology specifically addresses what mental health looks like and how to help heal ourselves when we are psychologically unwell. The answers that psychology offers are too often overlooked, underplayed, and maligned as the stuff of hippie peaceniks, feminists, or cowards when, in fact, *they are the only real and viable solution to our continued survival.* Why? Because the answers psychology holds take us off the battlefield with one another, and it is the climate of mental illness in America today that wants us to continue to do battle.

There are those who would argue that this is just the way it is and the way it has always been. People fight. They try to win whatever battle or argument they are in. There have always been those who have power and those who don't, the rich and the poor, the loved and the hated, and those in charge and those who must obey. Many people would argue that they can't fix everyone else's problems and it's okay to take care of themselves. And it may have always been this way. But we cannot allow ourselves to accept that it can go on this way unquestioned. We have reached a tipping point in terms of our ability to destroy ourselves with weapons of mass destruction, chemical pollution, and all the ways we have contributed to rapidly escalating climate change. But even more immediately, we are reaching a tipping point in losing connection to one another and a sense of our shared humanity. It is this broken bond of connection that allows us to terrorize and destroy others with no remorse. And so, without apology, I will say that the psychological makeup of those who ignore the threats to our planetary existence, target and scapegoat the vulnerable, and advocate war on any level as a tool of survival—their psychological makeup *mirrors exactly that of abusers in individual families*. And they are having the same devastating effects on all of us—and certainly on some more than others—that abusers have on their family members. *We are at the mercy, as a country, of abuse dynamics parading as ideological positions and beliefs*. The urgent climate change we must address immediately is the climate of abuse and neglect. This is both the bad news and the good news that psychology brings us.

Let's start with the bad news. The bad news is that abuse and neglect cause massive suffering. Abusers in families ostracize, blame, withhold necessities, exploit, physically and sexually assault, and take victims hostage. Abusive governing bodies do the same things. There are far too many examples to cite, but let's consider some that many of us are familiar with— like the rhetoric of former president Trump when he called immigrants rapists and thugs and enacted a policy of putting them in cages and kidnapping their children. Or we can look at police brutality aimed at Black people, as highlighted in this article from *The Imprint: Youth and Family News*. "Rodney King, Kathryn Johnston, George Floyd, Breonna Taylor, Atatiana Jefferson . . . Eric Garner, and Tamir Rice (all murdered by police) are just a few names of people who have notoriously suffered at the hands of our deleterious (abusive) systems. These senseless tragedies grow in numbers each day and cast an ominous shadow on the racially driven injustices and inequalities that are plaguing minorities, especially Black people."[2] And worse, the article went on to say many of the officers involved suffered no significant consequences. This is *institutionalized abuse* here in America. The abuser targets his victims in the light of day, and the Family of America too often either condones it, feels powerless to stop it, or is silenced in an effort to call it out. This is the Terror of the Situation.

But there is also good news, and we don't want to forget that. Number one, while there have always been power struggles in America between rich and poor, the loved and the reviled, there have also always been massive efforts at cooperation, community building, rehabilitation, and philanthropy, to name just a few of the ways we help rather than harm each other. Number two, both the oppressed and many of us who witness oppression continue to report it and try to stop it. Number three is that in the field of psychology, not only can we identify abuse dynamics, but we have a great deal of understanding of the origins of abuse, the psychological makeup of those who abuse others, and what is needed to interrupt the cycle of abuse and restore us to safety. This is the Hope for Our Country and really the hope for the world. It is the *only* hope. On the very farthest end of the continuum of individual violence is murder. On the very farthest end of national and international violence are atrocities like racial cleansing and nuclear war.

When an eighteen-year-old breaks into a school and kills twenty-one people, as a young man did in Uvalde, Texas, in May 2022, we do not have difficulty calling his actions criminal, and we are beginning to understand that he was mentally ill. We have begun to link the lethal behaviors of mass murderers to psychological disturbance, most often originating in early conditioning—abuse and neglect at home, bullying in school, and/or destructive role models in the community. In fact, it was later reported that the killer's mother had a drug problem, that he had suffered from a speech impediment but had never received special education services, and he had been bullied and possibly sexually abused as well. We are now beginning to put two and two together on the individual level, that the most violent and abusive among us very likely suffered abuse and neglect by other people. We are just beginning to understand that no one is born bad, a loser, or evil—that something happens to people that turns them in the direction of hatred and violence. We decry the lone shooter killing innocent children, and we are beginning to talk about how to identify these individuals and help them *before* they explode. This is exactly what we must now do with our institutions of power, our government, and leaders—identify those in power who behave like bullies and abusers. And we must look deeper into what is creating their drive to hate, exploit, and kill and stop them, just like we wish someone had stopped the Uvalde shooter. Stop them before any more intentional killings occur, any more *pre-meditated murder,* whether it is of a single Black man or thousands of civilians. We now have programs for conflict resolution in schools to stop bullying before it turns to violence, and mediation is now a common step in divorce settlements to help avoid violence and spare children the pain of warring parents. We need these same services in our most powerful governing bodies to bring us back from all the wars we are waging right here at home. Imagine for a moment that within our government, we hired therapists and mediators to help guide partisan politics out of conflict and toward compromise, agreement, and cooperation for the good of the Family of America!

Louder arguments, stubborn filibusters, bigger threats—and especially threats of violence—will not make us safer or better provided for. What will make us safer and ensure a viable future is psychological health—a mindset of commitment to the peaceful resolution of our issues and the motivation and skills to follow through. If enough people had taken it seriously that the eighteen-year-old Texan was nicknamed the school shooter long before he entered the elementary school, and if we had the best psychological help for him or at least identified the need to restrain him, there is a good chance those nineteen children and two adults would be alive today. Imagine how many thousands and millions of innocent people would be alive today if we got America to therapy—if we got our country the help it needs to stop the violence, hatred, and war. There is hope for us.

After I got my master's degree, I worked as co-director of a sexual abuse treatment program, had a private practice for over thirty years, and did many years of therapy myself. All this experience is what led me to the conclusion that we are living in a culture increasingly dominated by abuse from the bottom up and the top down. In my practice alone, seeing hundreds of people over the years, clients told me about murders they had witnessed as children, parents who raped them and beat them with wires and broken glass—tales so horrific they are difficult to digest. On the national level, we have given power to many people who behave just like the abusive adults my clients describe—leaders who authorize and justify the torture of prisoners and assault on peaceful demonstrators and wage wars around the world with no consideration for the untold numbers of soldiers and innocent civilians they send to their deaths.

We live in a curious climate in which abusive behaviors are openly displayed and widely reported, while at the same time, their impact is often minimized and denied. These are the same confusing and numbing dynamics found in abusive families. I was stunned (or perhaps not) to learn that US Representative Alexandria Ocasio-Cortez was sexually harassed on the steps of the Capitol by a man who called her his "favorite big booty Latina" and a "hot tamale" while accusing her of wanting to "kill babies."[3] Capitol police stood by and did not stop the harasser. She later said, "My experience here has given me a front-row seat to how deeply and unconsciously, as well as consciously, so many people in this country hate women. And they hate women of color." She was calling out abuse, and yet she was mocked by Tucker Carlson on the TV program Fox and Friends as he giggled in a high voice, "They're trying to kill me! They hate me! They just don't like women."[4] Regardless of political party, this is one of many dynamics of abuse—the victim calls for help and justice, and the response is dismissive and shaming. We must know that downplaying abuse and publicly demeaning the victim is a role model of behavior that we and our children are learning. When we are hurt, it is normal to cry out and expect help. Ignoring and mocking another's victimization is an *abnormal response* and a huge contributor to national mental illness.

The Big Picture for America

But I'd like to pause here and zoom out to the very big picture. I'm going to tell you the story of Estelle, who came to me for therapy many years ago. Shy and reserved, Estelle was a beautiful woman and a talented artist. Her work had recently been accepted at a gallery, and she volunteered teaching art to children. Estelle wasn't quite sure why she had come to therapy. Her boyfriend had urged her to was all she initially told me. After a few sessions, she haltingly showed me a small growth on her arm, and of course, my immediate reaction was to ask if she had seen a doctor. She said no, she didn't like doctors, and she didn't want any bad news. I urged her to go anyway. *If it's benign, great, but what if it needs treatment? Don't you want to find out if it needs to be removed?* To my amazement, she said no. I persisted. I was feeling all the concern Estelle should have been feeling, and I wanted to convey that to her through the urgency in my voice and the worried look on my face. I asked her why she had shown me the growth if she really didn't want to do anything about it. But she withdrew. It's nothing, she told me. It will probably go away. Perhaps she overwhelmed herself by telling me, or perhaps I overwhelmed her with my worry. I will never know. I only saw her one more time. Several years later, I ran into the client who had referred Estelle to me. With sadness, she told me Estelle had ignored the growth until it was too late; cancer had spread through her body, and she had passed away.

We are beautiful artists just like Estelle, with our spectacular creations, inventions, and discoveries over centuries and all the breathtaking acts of loving kindness, generosity, and service we perform every day. Yet within the very same body of our country also lie our fast-growing cancers— mass hatred, mass murder, and mass destruction of our planetary home. Like Estelle, we are at odds with ourselves. Estelle knew something was wrong, or she wouldn't have shown me the cancer. But another part of her needed to downplay the evidence as well as her fears. She retreated into denial. We, as a nation, are in the same position. The evidence that we are in deep trouble grows stronger daily. We show each other our "tumors," bombarding ourselves with images of suffering and destruction that all too quickly become the stuff of television, movies, books, and the basement fantasies of disturbed teenagers, lonely outcasts, and domestic terrorists. We are more blatant with ourselves about our symptoms than Estelle ever was. Yet there are conflicting voices inside our collective awareness, and like Estelle, we are masters at downplaying the seriousness of our condition. We could die from the cruelty and violence, but we don't have to.

Abuse, Neglect, and Mental Illness Go Together

We know many of the principles of what is needed to stop abuse and neglect and help heal both the injurers and the injured. We will explore this subject in detail as we continue. What we desperately need is a new understanding of the dynamics that both lead to abuse (including neglect) and perpetuate it that everyone can grasp. Abuse occurs on a continuum of severity. One dictionary definition describes abuse this way: to "treat a person with cruelty or violence, especially regularly or repeatedly." I will expand on the definition of abuse to say that abusive behaviors and dynamics are those which lead to alienation, failure to thrive, enforced isolation, self-harm, hatred, and violence toward others and the environment on a continuum to enslavement, assault, rape, torture, murder, and suicide.

Abuse and mental illness go together, whether issuing from a government official, a violent parent or spouse, or a mass shooter. We need to understand how critical it is to interrupt these dynamics and repair our human relations now. And we also need to know what we can each contribute, no matter how large or small the scope of our personal influence may be.

The assertion of this book is that restraint, safety, peace, and loving reconnection with one another are not ideological issues but the *anti-*

dotes to both abuse and to war. They are the only hope for America and for humanity, just as restraint and the restoration of safety, peace, and connection is the only hope for recovery for abusive individuals and their families. This is it! This is the answer lying hidden in plain sight! My commitment is to take everything I have learned as a psychotherapist out of the office and into the world, to make it accessible to everyone, and to create a national referendum for America to be in therapy before it is too late. This book is my contribution to how we can work together to do this now.

Many of us are still fueling the fires of division and war, and there is currently increased talk of civil war in America.[5] In October of 2022, the *New York Times* reported that just a few hours after the FBI searched former President Trump's Mar-a-Lago residence for classified government documents, posts on Twitter that mentioned "civil war" had soared nearly 3,000 percent. Similar spikes were seen across social media. Mentions of the phrase more than doubled on radio programs and podcasts, as measured by Critical Mention, a media-tracking firm. As of this writing, threats of civil war are still on the airwaves. This is just one tumor we are showing ourselves here in America. Will we downplay it like Estelle did, or will we take it seriously?

What would it mean to take it seriously? We get ourselves into therapy just like we would run, not walk, to find help if someone in our own family was threatening to come after us! It is a sign of pervasive mental illness sweeping America that would have anyone consider civil war a sane approach to dealing with conflict, and it is just as much a sign of mental illness in America that we have become numb to our most threatening symptoms. The real revolution that will save us from harm is a *psychological revolution*, which is everything we don't usually think revolution is. It requires that we evolve our understanding—that we realize just how dysfunctional the Family of America is and how desperately we need healing.

We Can All Help Heal Our Nation

Calling on my extensive experience working with hundreds of individuals, children, couples, and families for over thirty years, this book is the first of its kind to look at the current state of the nation through the deep lens of individual and family psychotherapy. By citing several case studies as well as professional observation, all the material in this book will be presented in a way accessible not only to those already familiar with psychology but also to those who have no psychological training or experience. The intention is to illuminate how we, as individuals, affect the largest national influencers and power holders and how they affect all of us. And I will explore with you what we can all do to change the course of our own history.

It is highly likely that some of what is covered in this book will meet fierce resistance as much as it may also bring insight and welcome relief. But as both a professional and a concerned citizen, as a mother and grandmother, I feel a longing and a duty to sound an alarm. We must know that extreme polarization, hatred, and violence are potentially lethal to us all *and that they can be stopped and prevented*. We can heal from the worst of their effects if we are armed with knowledge, understanding, and with the tools and values the very best psychology and psychotherapy can teach us.

The more we educate ourselves about what it will take to restore ourselves to safety, the greater the hope for our ultimate survival and "thrival." I wrote this book to help us heal our broken and dangerous human relations with the hope that we will each find our own way to contribute. For anyone who wants to end violence, who is deeply concerned that our children and all children everywhere will inherit a safe and habitable world, this book is for you.

Are you still with me, America? I ask.

Yes, she answers. *This is why I came to therapy. I believe in us. I want to hear where the hope lies.*

I believe in us too, I reply. *Let me offer you hope.*

Which leads me to share where the inspiration for this book came from.

Chapter 2

OUT OF THE OFFICE AND INTO OUR LIVES

T he idea for this book came to me many years ago. Like so many of us, I was called to do exactly the kind of work with others I needed to do myself. I needed therapy in the worst way when I was younger. So, when I first dared to talk to someone about my innermost world, it was a shock for me to discover that I was not born a flawed human being but that there were understandable reasons for the enormous pain I was in and how alone and unlovable I felt.

I grew up on a quiet suburban street in what appeared to be a normal family that valued education and classical music. We had plenty to eat, and I had dance and piano lessons. But something was not right with me, and I only knew that by sensing the "rightness" of other people, especially the girls around me who seemed so at home in their bodies and so happy with their boyfriends. I was consumed with desperately trying to hide an aching emptiness that I imagined showed anyway, living a life of solitary confinement within myself, pretending to be okay, though there was no memory of "okay-ness" anywhere inside me. When I was in my early twenties, I wrote and illustrated several children's books, but they really weren't for children. They were for me. The theme was always the same—I am a child who feels like she fell out of the sky. She doesn't know where she came from or where she belongs. She is lost, praying to be found. I had no idea where those stories came from.

By the age of forty, I was divorced, a single mother of three children, and I had gone back to school to get a master's degree in psychology and counseling. I was in a hypnotherapy class when we did a guided visualization back to a time before trauma or whatever incident had left a negative imprint in our psyche. I could not find my "before." What I got was a flash of a baby lying on a bassinet in a dark room. Terror and violation filled my body.

That was the beginning of a journey I had no idea I was about to make, a journey no one in my family had made as far as I knew. It's not like there wasn't plenty of pain buried in the wake of their lives as immigrants fleeing poverty and persecution in Eastern Europe in the early 1900s. But theirs seemed to be an outward journey, from one continent to another, fueled by the hope of reaching a promised land in America. The rest was unspoken. Mine, on the other hand, was to be an inward journey that was going to require speaking the unspeakable with no promised land in sight.

Most of that story is for another time. What matters here is that I finally uncovered the source of all that pain, and eventually, it set me free. Eventually . . . but not without making a terrifying descent into darkness, retrieving memories of sexual abuse that had sent my most essential self into hiding, and finally letting her scream it out of her system in a safe place.

The scattered, shattered pieces of myself began to reassemble. It might have been a mythic journey I made—a Greek goddess descends into the underworld and brings her radiant self into the light of day. But it didn't feel mythical at the time. It was slow and painful and frightening, and I had no expectation at all that there would be any kind of resurfacing into daylight. It was more like drowning and clawing my way up for air. That may sound overly dramatic, but that is the way it was. And all the while, I was working full time and writing my master's thesis on sexual abuse!

Why do I tell you all this? Because as I emerged and as I started a psychotherapy practice, met with clients, and heard so many stories just like my own, I understood that in my isolation, I was anything but alone. Back then, in the early 1990s, one in every four to five women was estimated to have experienced sexual abuse before the age of eighteen, and that could only be an estimate because there would have to be countless people like me who did not realize they'd been abused or who never reported their abuse to anyone. The big *Aha!*, which seems so obvious to me today, was that there are millions of people in this country and all over the world who are also a mystery to themselves, exactly as I was. Countless people who have no idea that their pain, anger, despair, isolation, or addiction can be traced back to traumas they remember and traumas they have buried, traumas that they have never had help for or knew there was help for or which they had been conditioned to believe they should be able to get over on their own. I was living a life in which my reactions and attractions and the terrible choices I sometimes made were a complete mystery to me, yet I felt I had so little control over any of it, which only brought more sadness and shame. I began to wonder: if that was my experience, then what is happening to the millions of untreated victims of sexual and physical assault in America (and worldwide), those suffering racial violence and discrimination, war and its aftermath, their children dead, their homes obliterated? I could only imagine, and I couldn't imagine at all.

What I did know is that the effects of untreated abuse are real, they are devastating, and they don't go away by themselves. I knew with certainty that there are millions of survivors among us who, right now, are overcome by feelings and behaviors that seem out of alignment with who they are, that are self-sabotaging and dangerous (just as mine had been), and that are the result of massive past and present abuse.[6] The United Nations reported in March 2022 that two billion people (one-quarter of the population of the world!) live in areas of ongoing conflict and that around the world, we are experiencing the highest number of violent conflicts since World War II. Another UN report stated that crime kills even more people than armed conflict—half a million people were killed around the world in 2017.[7] It is impossible to fully calculate the toll of human suffering left in the wake of such violence, but it must be something like the toll it took on me, multiplied millions and millions of times over.

It was only a short hop from that realization to getting the next big *Aha!*, which is that, as a country, *we are at the effects* of many untreated abuse survivors, personally and nationally. I also understood that we are at the effects of the traumas we have lived through as a country—the Civil War and 9/11 are two big examples—as well as the abuses we have inflicted as a country—the decimation of the Native Americans and the enslavement of Black people, again two obvious examples. And I understood that as we continue to scapegoat and terrorize part of our own populace, we are causing countless people to become symptomatic as I was symptomatic. I understood that, as a country, we are still in the dark about why we make some of the terrible choices we make and hurt ourselves and others, as I did before I learned about my past and my conditioning and had a chance to heal.

I saw how critical it is for *America to be in therapy* because we have become such an extreme danger to ourselves—our obsession with guns and weapons, our destruction of the environment, and our extreme polarization that puts so many marginalized populations and their supporters at risk for their lives. We are in danger because, as I will explore with you in detail, not all the injured among us are passive and constricted, as I was. Many are angry and acting out.

Violence is abuse. Rape is abuse. Hatred, scapegoating, destruction of a home or a homeland, slavery, deliberate exploitation, and war are all abuse. We are all part of the perpetration (not necessarily perpetrators), and we are all part of the victimization because we are all part of the Family of America. But the point, which I understand so well as both a client and a therapist, is to focus not on blame but on healing. This is the true gift that the principles of psychotherapy have for America: *psychotherapy does not have a partisan agenda.* It is not an ideology. It is not invested in who is right and who is wrong, who is good and who is bad. We may need to identify abuse and dysfunction and stop it the best we can, but the goal is never simply to retaliate, blame, or punish. The goal is to bring us back together in safety whenever possible and help us separate peacefully when it is not. For this reason, psychology offers America something that political parties and ideologies are not now able to do. This is the Hope for Our Country.

There has been no war that ends war. Containment may be an absolute necessity for the most violent among us and those we do not yet know how to restore to mental health, but punishment alone does not end crime or help people return to their communities with functional skills, a sense of belonging, or social responsibility. According to The Crime Report of 2021, seven in ten prisoners who were released in thirty-four states in 2012 were re-arrested within five years. Approximately 68% of those incarcerated in America return to prison within three years of release and 83% within nine years, the vast majority because both their emotional or mental state and the world they return to have not changed or been healed.[8]

Therapy for America means doing whatever it takes to address both our internal wounds and the external environment we create for one another. It means evolving our consciousness to a place where how we treat everyone is our priority. This is what I call revolutionary. Like my own journey, therapy for America is fundamentally about self-examination, unearthing formative influences that have shaped unhealthy beliefs and behaviors, and a willingness to learn something new. Evolution occurs when a life form meets a great resistance or threat to its well-being, in the face of which it must adapt and change to survive. Most life forms evolve of their own accord as the dictates of nature work on them. Eyesight and sense of smell sharpen, and resistance to drought or insect infestation increases. Or a species dies out if needed changes do not happen in time. We alone must *choose* to evolve—not our physical bodies but our consciousness—because the threat to our survival comes not from external nature but from our own human nature that is succumbing to impulses that are destructive. We are our own predator!

We Are in This Together

I don't know how to say this strongly enough or shout it loud enough. **What we do to one another, we do *to all of us*.** It is estimated that one in four girls are right now being molested in the United States and one in thirteen boys. Black people are imprisoned at six times the rate of white people. Our government is planning to spend approximately fifty billion dollars a year for the next ten years on nuclear weapons. People are suffering, and our focus is not on easing their pain! I never considered myself particularly political. I felt called to focus on the internal and interpersonal worlds. When my big *Aha!* moments occurred, I was surprised to discover that psychology, sociology, politics, and even history are not separate, and the evolution of my own consciousness would require me to speak about their impact on all of us.

Science is discovering the interdependence of all living things as well. We depend on pollinating insects to preserve our fruit and vegetable supply, and what one country puts as waste into rivers and oceans affects the viability of countless marine organisms we depend on for food. The list of our national and global interdependencies is endless. What we seem to miss is that we need each other to be emotionally and mentally healthy as much as we need to keep our oceans clean and not kill off the bees. The quality of how we meet our collective basic human needs has everything to do with whether we make it or not, whether someone becomes a killer or a loving parent. Cleaning up the psychological environment starts with determining if we are really eating good food and breathing clean air *in our relationships*. It means we look fearlessly at every area of our lives that creates the psychological toxicity that is potentially lethal to us all while we preserve all that is healthy for us. Said another way, we must evolve out of hatred and violence into love, care, and cooperation—from "low-tech" to "high-tech" human relations.

High- and Low-Tech Human Relations

We want all things high-tech, it seems—the latest phones, computers, and the fastest cars with all the bells and whistles. We pour billions into the most advanced weapons, yet somehow, we've lost sight of the need to upgrade the ways we relate to each other. That is why I have coined these terms—High- and Low-Tech Human Relations—so that we can bring the "technology" of human relations to the forefront. High-Tech Human Relations are what *heal* us from the hurt we have endured from other human beings, and they are also our best option for *preventing* further harm and violence. In a nutshell, High-Tech Human Relations are based in love, safety, connection, good boundaries, sharing, and a commitment to resolve conflict peacefully. Low-Tech Human Relations are the opposite. They are based in targeting and blame of others, violence, hatred, greed, alienation, and a belief in domination and suppression. There are many other characteristics of High- and Low-Tech Human Relations that I will share in more detail later, but this is the basic definition I use to distinguish healthy relationship dynamics from abuse dynamics.

To make this evolutionary leap to High-Tech Human Relations, we must understand the relationship between the individual and the family or group and the impact they have on each other. This is one of the great contributions of psychology and psychotherapy today. What we have learned is exactly what science is concluding in other realms. The part depends on and is influenced by the whole, and the whole depends on and is influenced by the part. Individual human beings can no longer be fully understood or healed apart from the level of wellness (or lack thereof) of the larger groups they interact with and depend on, and larger groups depend for their psychological well-being on the mental health of the individuals that make them up. America is as mentally ill or mentally well as its citizens, and those in positions of authority and control directly affect the mental health and well-being of every single one of us.

I would not have been able to make the journey out of my own darkness had I not understood that my symptoms were part of the bigger picture of the dysfunctional family I came from. I experienced sexual abuse *in my family*. I was not born depressed, anxious, or fearful. I became that way from abuse that happened behind closed doors. If we truly want our children to be safe from school shootings, if we want to stop living in fear of the next terrorist attack or a president who could impulsively launch nuclear weapons, we must dare to look at the mental ill-health of the country and its leadership and not focus solely on the most disturbed and dangerous individuals among us. This is what a family systems approach can provide from a *non-partisan* point of view.

As I shared with you, my own healing journey took me into some very dark and frightening places. I had night terrors and panic attacks. There were times I could barely leave my house. And I felt separated from even those I loved by a wall of endless pain. But I came out the other side. One of the many silver linings was that, as a result of my own inner work, I could go into the darkest places my clients needed to go as well. I'm not a big fan of darkness or the pain that lives inside it, but I know from my own experience there is no way around but through. I know there is the possibility of light at the end of the tunnel if we are willing to make the journey. I know that for myself and for the people I have been so blessed to work with. And now I am offering that same hope to America.

What you're saying seems counter to so much of what we've been told, America says. *We're taught to buck up. We've made not crying into a virtue. But at the same time, none of that has worked. The pain of the people only grows. Tell me more.*

A Family Systems Approach

Family systems theory burst on the scene of psychology like a meteor crashing into earth. It turned us all on our psychological axis, upending a whole set of assumptions that kept us confined, like prisoners, to an outdated belief that we are all islands in a vast human sea, each of us solely responsible for every thought, feeling, and belief we have and every behavior we exhibit, each of us solely responsible for whether we sink or swim. We know now that we are all directly affected and shaped by the health and well-being (or lack thereof) of the whole family. To understand the individual, we must understand the psychological environment that is shaping and conditioning their beliefs, feelings, and behaviors. If a plant is wilting, we look to see if it has enough water, light, and mineral-rich soil. We know what it needs from its environment to be healthy and grow. This is what the birth of family systems theory did for our understanding of what is needed for our mental and emotional health and what conditions contribute to the most psychologically ill among us.

No child is born a bully or physically violent (barring biological or neurological diversity). When a child exhibits such behaviors, we now know that the most likely cause is pain and distress in the family. I have learned through experience with countless clients that many of our most destructive and antisocial behaviors are a direct result of abuse, neglect, or addiction and other issues within the family or of painful conditions affecting the family from the larger environment—poverty, discrimination, oppression, upheaval, and war. Without this understanding, we are bound to a belief in blame, shame, judgment, overuse of medication, punishment, and further isolation, all of which perpetuate themselves. Blame, shame, and punishment do not cure. They are part of the disease!

Our whole approach to emotional healing has changed as a result of understanding family dynamics. Even if we are working with individuals, we look deeply into their family history to help them make sense of where they are stuck or hurting in the present. When treating children, we now bring in parents and siblings and look at what the child is learning that is healthy or not and what part they are required to play in the whole family scenario. Without this revelation, we were unable to provide the help we can give today. We can identify High- and Low-Tech Human Relations in the family dynamic not through a lens of blame but through a lens of understanding what hurts people the most and what is needed to heal dysfunction and abuse. Healing the family is the key to healing the individual.

What would family therapy look like for America? We usually start with a family history. While it is not in the scope of this book to try to summarize the complexity of American history, for the purposes of this book, we can identify that the original settlers came here for many different reasons—to escape religious persecution and for religious freedom, to have new opportunities to get rich, and as an alternative to debtor's prison for some and from imprisonment for Scots and Irish captured in wars with England. Many of those seeking to get rich went to Jamestown, which was also the area where the first slaves from Africa came ashore. Others released from prison in exchange for settling in America went to Georgia. The point is for us to be aware that Americans were a diverse group from the beginning, and different populations settled in different places. Over many hundreds of years, people from all over the world have come to America—some against their will, others seeking asylum from poverty, persecution, and war, and some to get rich or for adventure. They came from different racial backgrounds and a wide variety of religious, political, cultural, gender, and other beliefs and practices. They also brought with them both their past traumas and their strengths and skills. And from the beginning, there were people already here, the Native

Americans who, in the big picture, we did not accept as the legitimate inhabitants of the land and who we did our best to subjugate and destroy.

If therapy does nothing more than identify our origins and take us back to both our pain and our potential, we have already come a long way. Together with all our strengths and desire for political and religious freedom, we also bring with us *the pain we fled and the pain we inflicted.* There is no real healing without understanding both the traumas we carry and the gifts we have yet to fully manifest. In this sense, our history is undeniably a part of who we are. And, just as it is in an individual family, we all have our own version of what that history is and how it has impacted each of us. We need to hear all voices to begin to get a more accurate picture of what has conditioned us as individuals and as a country; just as in family therapy, we let everyone speak, and we learn how to listen.

What psychology tells us is that when some populations are thriving and well-fed, and others are despised, deprived, or assaulted, both in the present and historically, we must look at the climate of the country and ask ourselves why these discrepancies are so. In a healthy family, we do not feed one child and starve another. We do not put one in a warm bed and the other out in the cold. In fact, we have lost, or perhaps never really had, a sense of America as a family unit. I believe we have not reconciled what are individual rights, state's rights, and the obligations of a federal government to decide on and look out for the good of everyone, and so we tolerate the vast discrepancies in how people are treated as inevitable or justified. This is where a family systems approach will help us understand what is happening in the Family of America and what to do to address our most threatening symptoms.

The principles and rules of how we live and work together—and work out our disagreements—as states and communities in relationship with the federal government are outlined in Article 4 of the Constitution, just as any family might have basic ground rules. At the same time, in any family, people change and grow, and the larger social networks and external conditions they must adapt to change as well. These changes require a constant re-examination of needs and renegotiation of the terms of relationship. The challenge to family relations, for both individual families and for the Family of America, comes when we don't agree, and we have many issues we don't agree on in the Family of America—the rights of minorities and immigrants, abortion, gun laws, equal pay for equal work for women, voting rights and laws—the list is long, and the issues are fraught. These are the issues at play in partisan politics that are presented as an ideological divide. Family systems theory helps us break the trance of ideology by showing us that it is not only the issues themselves that present a problem. It is how we come together, or not, to try to work out our disagreements that is the problem.

The explosive conflict over slavery and state versus federal authority resulted in the Civil War, in which it is estimated that 620,000 men died in the line of duty.[9] We are faced with the same challenge that the North and South faced: we can employ our best conflict resolution skills to settle our differences, or we can keep talking about and inciting another civil war. We can commit to High-Tech Human Relations and nonviolent conflict resolution, or we can continue with the Low-Tech Human Relations that justify hatred and the potential slaughter of thousands of innocent men, women, and children. As the Family of America, how much do we value human life? I believe our greatest challenge today is to find a way to handle conflict that is safe and constructive for everyone, *and* we must look at the issues we are fighting over and try to understand if our positions are in line with High-Tech Human Relations, which offer the healthiest environment for the American people. To be overly simplistic, if we are fighting over whether we should be allowed to kill defenseless Black men or teargas peaceful demonstrators, we might want to look at the wisdom of the argument in the first place.

We must ask ourselves: do we respect one another and support all members of the Family of America to thrive? This is what we expect and want for ourselves in our individual families, is it not? Can we learn to tolerate our differences while we hold to structures and ground rules that *we all abide by* to resolve conflict, stay related, and cooperate with one another? These values lie at the heart of High-Tech Human Relations. To the extent that we do not employ these values as a country, we are operating on Low-Tech Human Relations, which, on a continuum of escalating scapegoating, withholding, and violence, are the characteristics of abusive families.

A climate of abuse and neglect in an individual family creates mental illness. It creates explosive anger, fear, subservience, and aggressive, violent behaviors in many people. And yes, we may know people who have survived horrible abuse and have thrived anyway. These survivors are some of our most inspiring heroes and heroines! (I will explain later about what makes escape from the cycle of abuse more possible for some.) The human spirit can be indomitable, and thank goodness for that! But I am here to say that the threat posed to all of us is serious to the point of life-threatening when too many people have no access to help, and some are abused beyond our ability to help them recover. Looking at gun violence alone in the United States, in 2022, there were 647 mass shootings and an estimate of over 44,000 deaths due to gun violence.[10] We are not safe.

We created guidelines for states and the central government to both cooperate and navigate conflicting needs, just like any family does, but we're not following our own rules! The January 6 insurrection is a perfect example. There was a great controversy about the election results that named Joe Biden the winner, replacing Donald Trump. Although there was no evidence of voter fraud, many Trump supporters tried to stop the certification of Biden's win. Thousands of people invaded the Capitol, destroying property and threatening lives. Vice President Pence was being called upon to overturn the election, but he declared, "My oath to support and defend the Constitution constrains me from claiming unilateral authority to determine which electoral votes should be counted and which should not . . . The presidency belongs to the American people . . . It is the people's representatives who review the evidence and resolve disputes through a democratic process."[11] He was trying to uphold the family rules of the nation even though it meant he was voted out of office. Yet it took then-president Trump, who had sworn to uphold the Constitution, over two hours to call in the National Guard to stop the violence. Five people died as a result.

So, how do we repair the Family of America? I want to tell you more about what breaks the container of safety in a family that is breaking the container of safety in our country, not for the sake of blaming anyone but so that we know what needs repairing here in America and how we can all participate in repairing it. Calling out abuse on any level in order to heal is necessary, but it is not the same as calling it out to punish the haters or exact revenge. It can feel like a slippery slope because we may have intense feelings about the injustices done and the pain people have endured that make it very difficult to hold a light of healing around uncovering all that has hurt us.

But that's what good therapy does, I tell America. *It holds the light of healing around our worst pain.*

I take her hand. America looks to the side and behind her as if worried someone is listening in on our conversation.

There are people who don't know I'm here, she whispers. *People who would be upset about what I'm telling you and angry that I am talking to you at all.*

It's okay, I tell her. *Everything we say is confidential.*

Okay, she says. *Go on.*

Chapter 3:
THE FAMILY OF AMERICA DYNAMICS

So many people today are asking why, as a country, we have become so polarized, why extremism is on the rise, and why we are continuing to ravage the earth when we can't live without her. While there are many angles from which to answer these questions—the impact of industrialization, the loss of close tribal connections, the role of the media in fueling conflict, and the ongoing difficulties between gender, racial, and economic groups, to name just a few—I will highlight some of the most important understandings psychology can give us about why we are here so that we do not have to remain a mystery to ourselves any longer.

I want to show you how family dynamics work, I tell America. *I'll tell you the story of Michelle, a twelve-year-old girl I saw for therapy many years ago.*

Michelle was referred to me for therapy because she was wetting the bed and having nightmares. I asked her parents to come in first and give me an overall sense of the history and what they thought might be upsetting Michelle. Everything was fine, as far as they knew. She just seemed more withdrawn lately and didn't want to have friends over. I asked if anything was going on at home that might be bothering her. Her parents said no, there was nothing out of the ordinary. I asked them to bring the whole family to our next session, and we did what is called a family sculpture, in which each person creates a scenario of their idea of what the family looks like. Then, they tell each person to say one sentence. Michelle, her two sisters, and her parents took turns setting up their scenes. Mother, father, and both sisters created benign scenarios of the family making breakfast, kids doing homework, and so forth. *What's wrong with this picture?* I thought to myself. Michelle went last. She placed her father on one side of the room and her mother facing him on the other. The sisters were off to one side. Michelle instructed her parents to point at one another and yell at each other to stop their drug use! The cat was out of the bag.

It was a painful moment for all of them, to say the least. And it was especially awkward for Michelle's parents. I asked the children to go into the waiting room and turned to Michelle's parents. They were angry at one another and wanted to blame, but I stopped them with all the calm and gentleness I could muster. I told them Michelle had done them a great favor. "Why?" they asked, incredulous. "Because you are both miserable, and this is the only way she knows to tell you she is feeling your pain," I answered.

Michelle's symptoms were immediately understandable in a way that they would not have been had I not had a window into the family issues she was trying her best to cope with. It was clear that the real help for Michelle would have to come from her parents addressing their addiction issues. There was nothing wrong with Michelle! She was having a normal reaction to a very unhealthy situation. But if we were to try to understand Michelle apart from what was going on around her, we might be tempted to blame or shame her for wetting the bed, give her consequences, promise rewards, or take her to a doctor to see if she had a physical problem. Yet the truth was that the bed-wetting was the tip of the iceberg of the emotional violence raging in her home—the only part that showed. And the emotional violence raging between her parents was only the tip of the iceberg of deeply buried traumas in both parents' early lives. Both had come from raging households, and Michelle's mother had been severely physically abused as a child.

Just like Michelle, if I had any idea when I was younger that my pain and inner isolation were the result of something terribly amiss in my family, not in myself, I might have had a very different life.

We are beginning to look below the surface now, way below the tip of the iceberg of violence to the whole structure that holds it up. It is just now becoming more commonly known that people often express family pain in highly destructive ways—from physical and sexual violence to addictions to bullying and stealing, cutting, suicide, and murder. The list is long. And there are less obvious ways that family pain is expressed, such as in pervasive depression and anxiety, obsessions, isolation, unrealistic expectations, and in rigid, intolerant belief systems.

We are also now beginning to identify issues of abuse and neglect related to the absence of appropriate limits and boundaries. Not all abuse takes the form of physical, sexual, or verbal violence, discrimination, or ostracizing. Some people were never given appropriate limits and boundaries to begin with. They were never taught that other people's needs, feelings, or well-being matter. They grow up feeling they are the most important one in the room and that others are there primarily to serve their needs and desires.

My client Benny's story is one of outrageous over-empowerment, a story vitally important for America today because individuals and institutions that are over-empowered or all-powerful and have no effective limits and nothing to stop them from treading on the bodies, property, rights, and well-being of others are dangerous. They can and do become abusive, if not murderous.

Benny was a six-year-old who was acting more like a two-year-old. He had tantrums, refused to follow directions at school, and had no friends. I met with Benny's parents and learned that he was almost uncontrollable at home. He refused to go to bed at night and kept everyone up. Most recently, he had chased his sister around the house with a knife and then fell and cut himself. A troubled child on his way to becoming a criminal? Not really. In truth, there was nothing wrong with Benny. The problem was in the family system. Benny's parents were lovely people, but they didn't know how to say no to Benny. While they clearly loved their children, they had no sense of how to make boundaries with Benny. They were afraid of his tantrums, so they gave him whatever he wanted, hoping he would stop screaming or throwing things. They didn't realize they were, in fact, teaching him that the more he screamed, the more he would get what he wanted. Benny was running the entire family, and he was a very unhappy child. His sister did her best to stay away from him. Benny needed to be stopped! He was not internalizing self-control. His parents were so busy trying to avoid his outbursts, so unable to tolerate their own distress from his endless tantrums, they were not teaching him that other people had needs and rights. He was not learning to tolerate his own distress at not getting everything he wanted. The result was that Benny was insecure and increasingly entitled to whatever he wanted. The combination of insecurity and over-empowerment resulted in Benny becoming what some people would have called a little monster, a very unlikeable, dangerously aggressive little boy—through no fault of his own! It is frightening to think of the dangerously aggressive adult he might have become had his family not sought help.

I didn't work with this family very long. Benny's parents got it. They learned to say no to Benny with firmness, not violence. They understood that making limits was the most loving thing they could do for him. They sat resolutely outside his bedroom door while he screamed when they put him to bed. They put him in time-out when he hit his sister. And they learned to tolerate their own distress, perhaps the hardest job of all for them, but they were so alarmed by how violent he had become that they persevered, and it didn't take long for Benny to calm down, go to bed, and stop the tantrums. His teacher said he had become a different child at school. He was getting along with other children and making friends. Early intervention in the family dynamic (rather than labeling Benny a problem child) changed Benny's life.

A lack of appropriate boundaries can be as destructive to the psyche and as symptom-producing as rage and violence. Boundaries are what define where I end and others begin, where what I want and need meets what others want and need, and where we learn that everyone's needs and everyone's well-being matter. Good boundaries help teach us not only that we will not always get everything we want, but they teach us how to tolerate those limitations without acting out or turning against ourselves. Benny's parents were passive and helpless with their child, and that allowed him to believe he was entitled to whatever he wanted with no regard for others. As a result, he became a tyrant. He wasn't born that way. He became that way. He was healed when the family system was healed, when those in rightful positions of power used their authority for the good of both the individual and the family. Benny's parents may very well have saved him from a lifetime of loneliness covered over with aggression, with goodness knows what outcomes for those around him.

Abuse and neglect in families take many forms. I will not be able to name them all. Some are overt, and some are subtle or hidden. None of us relates to others—spouses, children, friends, and colleagues—perfectly. We all have our less-than-stellar moments. We yell or let our kids get away with too much or are unavailable when we need to be present. This is the human condition. When we are operating more or less within the realm of High-Tech Human Relations—with love, caring, cooperation, and nonviolent conflict resolution and with the goal of staying related, even with our lapses—that's pretty much as good as it gets as far as I can see.

There are many loving, law-abiding, caring people living peaceful, constructive lives, doing their best to take care of their loved ones, serve others, and offer their gifts and talents. Good therapy identifies the strengths we have as individuals because these are the resources we call upon to face our pain, and these are the strengths we grow when we have a chance to heal. Good therapy for America also remembers our strengths as we summon the courage to face the abuses we are suffering and the suffering we have caused. It's when the family dynamic tips over into Low-Tech Human Relations and is run by violence, shame, and blame, is ostracizing and rigid, or no boundaries are set that we should be concerned. The prevalence of alarmingly Low-Tech Human Relations that I observe in both individual families and in our nation is what I hope with all my heart will put us all on high alert. I hope it helps us see that if we really want to understand those who are beating their spouses and children, dying of overdoses by the thousands, leaving death threats for elected officials, buying assault weapons, storming the Capitol to attack members of Congress, and joining extremist and terrorist organizations here and abroad, then we must begin to examine not only their earliest conditioning in their families but also the conditioning coming from the very largest family systems they are a part of—in their workplaces, communities, and in the country as a whole.

The Microdynamics of Abuse

Let's look at the tactics of abusers and the effects on their victims on micro and macro levels. Though I will be unsparing about how I see abuse dynamics playing out in our country, please remember that the goal is to bring understanding and healing, not more hatred and blame. I will start by saying that the line between the abusive spouse who beats, tortures, or murders his partner and children and the despot who persecutes a minority or bombs a city of innocent men, women, and children—*that line is an illusion.* There is *no line* between them. The justifications abusers use to feel righteous about the pain they inflict on others are the very same justifications the most powerful authorities and governing bodies use to discriminate against, exploit, subjugate, and kill those they wish to control and take from. **All the ways we avoid recognizing that the actions of abusive individuals and abusive power institutions are equally criminal and insane is one of the greatest challenges we face here in America and around the world.** And yet, to own this terribly confronting truth is exactly what will pull us back from the edge of our own extinction.

We have only to look at the recent policy of forcibly separating immigrant children from their parents and putting them in cages. Or our history of taking Native American children from their parents and communities and forcing them to abandon their language and Native identity. Or how we enslaved Black people, tortured them, and sold their children away from them. What member of our own communities would be allowed to do such things to their own or anyone else's children and not only not be prosecuted but also not be considered mentally ill? Hundreds of thousands of helpless Americans reacted with horror and outrage to pictures of children huddled in cages, but that did not immediately stop the kidnapping. The resounding response from the therapeutic community was not only horror and outrage but a very clear message that the lives of these children were being irrevocably damaged, to say nothing of the lasting devastation of their parents. The Guardian reported that under the Trump administration, over five thousand children were separated from their parents at the border—the youngest four months old—and that many were suffering severe mental health disorders even after reunification.[12] Reuters reported in February of 2023 that almost one thousand children separated by Trump have not been reunited with their parents.[13] One boy said of his detention, "The way I have been treated makes me feel like I don't matter, like I am trash." And a little girl reported, "They sent me to a room with other children. I saw my mom, and she was chained at her feet, her waist, and her hands, and I was crying."[14]

It is a disturbed state of mind that would advocate and implement such treatment of other human beings, especially children. It is a disturbed state of mind that does not want to recognize the lasting pain and suffering of those so cruelly treated. Yes, there are many arguments for extreme measures. Some might say we have to deter immigrants because we can't take care of all those people, some people are just bad, and they deserve what they get, or we must use force to defend ourselves against our enemies. Surely, there is a legitimate case for war, many people would argue. And there will always be an argument for justified self-defense, but what I want to explore with you is **how to stop the cycle of violence,** not continue to justify it when anger and conflict have escalated out of control. In the big picture, when self-defense could mean the extinction of much of life as we know it, don't we want to get that weapon out of our hands before we have convinced ourselves we have the right to use it?

When we advocate and condone violence and abuse on any level, we are perpetuating the very same dynamics that create abusers in the first place while also rendering more and more people powerless to stand up to it. Our current national (and international) capacity for war is not only mass abuse; it is premeditated murder that is now on a continuum to global homicide-suicide. ICAN reported that in 2020, the United States increased its nuclear spending by $1.4 billion, bringing its total to $37.4 billion. America and Russia own nearly 90% of the world's nuclear weapons, and America has yet to commit that it will not use nuclear weapons first.[15] This should be an alarm ringing in all our ears. In a 2022 report by CBS, a large-scale nuclear war between the US and Russia would kill 360 million people immediately and more than five billion from starvation because soot from the blasts would cool world temperatures by over fifty-eight degrees Fahrenheit.[16] But I'm not sure the average citizen knows what we are playing with when we talk about war or the use of nuclear weapons.

Literally at this very moment in my writing, an email popped up on my screen reporting yet another fatal mass shooting here in America. Where do we begin to end this? **I am here to talk about the prevention of violence in our country and issuing from our country, just like we work toward the prevention of family violence in our psychotherapy offices. When we focus on prevention, we must look deeper into the causes.** What we are doing now clearly isn't working. The field of psychology will help us connect the dots between abuse and neglect in the family and abuse and neglect nationally. We were all children once in the families that raised us, and it is in those families that our primary conditioning took hold. The Uvalde shooter was a newborn baby once. He wasn't born a murderer. Something happened to him. We must look at the families we are all born into—our individual families and the Family of America. Are they more loving and connected, or are they more abusive and neglectful? Because it is our children who will inherit the nation and the earth we leave them, having been infused with the mental health and coping strategies they absorbed from us in our homes and in our country. The New York Times reported in June 2022 that six of the nine deadliest shootings in America since 2018 were committed by people twenty-one years old and younger, calling it a "disturbing new pattern."[17]

In the early part of my practice as a psychotherapist, I worked exclusively with children. Ninety-nine percent of all children I saw were brought to therapy because they were having difficulty adjusting to the divorce of their parents. At the time I met Justin, he was a blonde six-year-old with a splatter of freckles across his nose. His parents reported that he had been a happy, outgoing little boy, but now he was withdrawn and having trouble making friends. His parents were in the middle of a nasty divorce. Justin spent his entire first session arranging plastic army men in neat rows facing each other, poised for battle. Off to one side, he built a wall of blocks, and behind that wall, he placed one army man. I asked him to tell me about his scenario, and he told me it was a war. "If you were one of the army men, which one would you be?" I asked. He immediately pointed to the man standing behind the wall. "I don't want to fight," he said. "How's he feeling back there?" I asked. "Scared," he said. "What's the wall?" I asked. "It's a jail," Justin answered. He didn't want to play out the actual war. He just wanted to show me what the divorce was like for him. His parents were still fighting over custody, often in front of him. Justin's play showed me that he was trying to get away from the battle but that retreating also felt like imprisonment. He was in a no-win situation.

The real work, the work that could make all the difference in Justin's life, was with his parents, just as it had been for Michelle. His parents were so caught up in their own pain they didn't realize the impact they were having on their son. It was my job to re-interpret back to them what Justin needed from them to feel safe and come out of hiding. I could point the way, but his parents would have to do the hard work of changing the way they were relating to each other, settle their divorce, and stop the verbal and emotional violence. They had to end the tug-of-war over their son and make it safe for him to love them both. Until I met with them, Justin's parents had no idea their hostility toward one another had anything to do with their son's withdrawal. Many parents are in the same boat—so consumed by their own pain and struggles (divorce or not) that they do not consider the ripple effect of unresolved conflict on their children. Justin's parents learned to talk out of his earshot, not say terrible things about each other to him, and deal with their upset feelings in another setting—imperfectly, to be sure, but much better. Eventually, Justin's parents agreed on a custody arrangement they could both live with. Was the situation perfect? No. Justin still suffered from his parents' breakup, as most children do. His mother was angry and bitter, and I referred her for her own therapy. Divorce, even without major conflict, is traumatic for many (if not most) adults and children. But at least the pain of being a helpless pawn in his parents' struggles with each other could be ameliorated for Justin, and that helped him feel safer and more secure.

Justin's story is just one of many, and it isn't the worst by far. I saw children of divorce who were forbidden to see one of their parents, forced into a new stepfamily but never accepted, or even put in foster care when their parents' fighting became violent. All these children were highly symptomatic—one little boy chewed his shirt collar to shreds and developed a tic; some had night terrors or tantrums, bullied other children, wouldn't go to school, or lived in constant fear that a parent would die. Children like Justin, who get a chance to heal, are in the minority. We will never know how many more are suffering now from these and worse instances of family pain—abandonment, addiction, physical and sexual abuse, and gun violence. We need to ask ourselves who these children will grow up to become as partners and parents themselves if there is no help for them and their families. How will they cope with relationships and the stressors of adulthood?

The Macrodynamics of Abuse

The macro level of conflict and devastation is a whole other story, with consequences that are exponentially greater, globally far-reaching, and much more difficult to treat. Here in America, we want to understand that the conflicts deliberately fueled and the wars we then wage on one another—white against Black, men against women, straight against LGBQT, rich against poor, one religion against another, conservative against liberal—are profoundly affecting masses of people, some of whom become profoundly symptomatic. We are living in a national family environment that believes in and promotes our separation and divorce from one another with no commitment to resolution. We've enacted segregation in schools and businesses, and even though the laws have changed, racial discrimi-

nation and racially motivated violence are alive and well. We are in conflict about whether people with gender differences can marry or be in
the service or whether they even have the right to be served in public
businesses. Legitimate American citizens of foreign ancestry are brutally
attacked and screamed at to go home. And all these people have children who are, by default, if not directly, being abused in the Family of
America. These are the people some believe are undeserving, inferior, or
innately bad, but they don't go anywhere. They suffer the same terrible
consequences as Justin, only the guns fired on them, the guns they fire,
and the prisons they are confined in are real.

Looking through the lens of what makes a healthy family and what
are the characteristics of abusive and neglectful families, it is clear we
have created the same separation affecting millions of people around the
world. Colonization, presented as expansion, was, in fact, a way we separated whole nations from caring, cooperation, and protection in order to
take from them, and it opened the door to massive abuse—rape of land,
resources, women, and children. It forced entire populations to be part of
a "family" they did not want and that did not want them, except insofar
as there was something to be taken from them. They were forced to be
the neglected child in a "family" that did not and does not to this day
see or treat them as equals. We can no longer operate on the assumption
that 'might equals right' when might manifests as theft from and abuse
of other people any more than we would consider it right for a powerful
neighbor to break into our home and take our car or our children.

At the same time, I am not denying that there are as many guns being
held to our national head as we are holding to the heads of other nations
around the world. We and all our children suffer to the extent that those
threats invade our psyches and our lives. But if we look at Justin's parents
or any warring couple, what is needed to create a whole new future is for
one of them to put their weapons down and commit to finding resolution.
Peace and safety must start somewhere with someone, whether an indi-

vidual or a nation, willing to put their weapons down and do exactly what we expected Justin's and Michelle's parents to do, which is to work it out for the sake of their children if not for themselves.

Power Struggles

I know what I am saying is confronting for a country that prides itself on its military strength and capabilities. So, stay with me because if there is anything good family counseling has taught us, it is that no one wins a power struggle. I'm right, and you're wrong; I'm good, and you're bad; my needs are more important than your needs—these are the power struggles that tear people apart. Barring biochemical impairment or the need for physical restraint, the reason no one wins a power struggle is that we lose relationship. I may dominate you and get what I want or shame you into submission, but I have lost relationship with you, and you have lost safe connection with me. The biggest fallout from continuous power struggles is that our care and concern for the impact we have on other people is dimmed or lost in our investment in winning. Then the door is wide open for exactly the kind of aggression that was causing Justin and Michelle so much pain—hatred, rage, assault, and the desire for revenge, conquest, and possession of what does not belong to us. On the national and international scene, these impulses are armed and deadly. Armed and deadly. This is the Terror of the Situation. The Hope for Our Country (and our world) is that we make a conscious choice for nonviolent conflict resolution rather than the continued power struggles that put us all on the brink of extinction.

Justin's parents were and always would be his parents. They didn't have to love each other or spend time together, but they needed to maintain a cooperative relationship for Justin's sake. Individual family members, Americans, and world citizens—we are all neighbors, and we are parents to all the children in the world. The more we lose relationship with one another (even if we need to be cautious), the less we will care about our impact on each other and all future generations. The less we care at the national and international levels, the more we keep the door open to war. Period. Our children will be the ones to inherit this earth (if there is an earth to inherit). Together, they will make up the social, emotional, political, and cultural environment they and their children must navigate to survive. They will be the stewards of the earth itself. And there will be no getting away from each other, no divorce possible from planet earth. Can we bring ourselves to therapy now, while we have time?

Someone must lead the way. In personal relationships, one person can change the whole dynamic by getting out of the power struggle. Like a dance partner, if one person changes their step, the other cannot dance the old dance with them. We can learn how to exit the power struggles we have with one another here in America and with other countries and peoples all over the world if we are brave enough to take what we can learn from psychology and point the way to an initiative for world peace.

Woodrow Wilson held that light for us, but we did not implement it. He proposed a fourteen-point plan for world peace in 1918 at the end of World War I. Wilson outlined what he believed caused world war—secret treaties, increased weapons production, and unresolved issues related to colonization, among other things. He proposed commitment to self-determination for oppressed peoples and the creation of an organization for world peace and security, which became part of what was called the League of Nations.[18] It was, however, not to be. The US Senate did not vote to join the League of Nations. Wilson predicted there would be another world war if the United States did not participate, and indeed there was. After World War II, we tried again with the founding of the United Nations, which helps end conflict and addresses humanitarian needs. US support of the UN has been strong historically but has shifted in the recent political climate.

We face the same pressing issues today—ending conflict and addressing humanitarian needs here at home. Let's start, like all good therapy starts, with ourselves. Ending conflict and addressing the humanitarian needs of Americans are part of High-Tech Human Relations, the antidote to abuse and violence.

Caught in the Middle

Carol's story is a great example of what ordinary people like you and me can do. Five-year-old Carol's parents got divorced after her father, Jim, had an affair with her mother Ann's best friend. Jim and his new love married and had a baby. Soon after, Carol began talking baby talk at pre-school and cried easily. Long story short, Carol's mother had forbidden her to talk about her father or his new family, and her father was blissfully unaware that Carol was caught between her parents. Once a bubbling little girl, she was now subdued and regressing to a toddler state.

Again, the work was with the parents. I asked Ann and Jim and Jim's new wife to meet with me to make some agreements for Carol's sake. I was quite impressed that they came. It is a session I will never forget. The three of them sat side by side on my couch, with Jim in the middle. They "got it" that Carol needed to feel free to love and be loved by every-one. No anger flared. No blame got hurled in any direction. For that hour anyway, all three adults considered Carol first and agreed to everything we discussed.

This was High-Tech Human Relations at work. **High-Tech Human Relations do not deny the ruptures, pain, anger, or resentments; they offer a way to come back to repair and connection for the sake of all concerned, especially the children, and they highlight the incredible gains to be had from doing so.**

Carol's symptoms died down almost immediately. Did Ann and Jim do everything we discussed perfectly? I highly doubt it, not because I think less of them but because progress in personal growth is usually two steps forward, one step back. A divorce that involves such deep betrayal cannot be easy. But part of being an adult means that no matter what our feelings and pain may be, we cannot justify acting out. We must also take seriously our impact on those we have the most influence, power, and control over. Many of us simply don't know this, and we need help to learn it. Therapy helped Carol's parents gain a new understanding of why she had become symptomatic and what they could each do to help her. Even if they dropped the ball, which I imagine they did many times, they had a way back whenever they could remind themselves of their child's welfare. This might be as good as it gets.

And the beautiful thing is, many of us are doing what Carol's parents did. NPR Politics Broadcast reported that here in America, there is a non-profit group called Braver Angels that puts on Red/Blue Workshops all over the country to bridge the divide between Republicans and Democrats. Hundreds of such groups are committed to helping people listen to one another in a space of safety and civility.[19] Betsy Harwood, a participant, said, "I think that what we see here in this room is the true America. It's a group of people who can get together and talk politely with each other and understand each other. It's not what we see on the news or what we see on social media. That's not the real America."[20]

If we choose, nothing can stop us from sitting down together and working it out. We can be the Braver Angels. If not us, who?

America looks hopeful.

Yes, how inspiring that ordinary people are taking it on themselves to enact what our government officials should be modeling, she says. *We can do this. We just need to understand what is at stake and what we can gain. The Braver Angels of America could be all of us, released from the no-win of choosing sides against each other.*

Chapter 4:

THE DYNAMICS OF ABUSIVE FAMILIES

As the Braver Angels ourselves, let's look together inside the body of America with the same courage and spirit of exploration that those who first opened a corpse did to find healing for the still living.

There are very specific dynamics typical of abusive family systems, I tell America. *We're going to look through this lens now to understand the dynamics of the Family of America. But remember, the diagnosis by itself may be frightening, but it leads us to the cure.*

America shifts uncomfortably in her chair, but she is still making eye contact with me. *Go on,* she says. *I'm with you.*

Abusers Blame Their Victims for the Abuse

A hallmark of abusers is that they blame their victims for the abuse. They target one or more and attribute inferiority or other undesirable characteristics to them as justification for the abuse. This is what happened to my forty-five-year-old client, Jean, a successful landscape architect who was suffering from severe anxiety. She had recently moved away from her father and was being plagued with angry phone calls from him, insisting she send more money home. Jean had been severely beaten by her father throughout childhood. He told her she was ugly and stupid, and he had forced her sisters to hold her down while he hit her. He had even slapped Jean as an adult. Jean never married and believed she was unlovable. She believed she must have deserved the abuse her father heaped on her. But Jean kept sending her father money, and she went overboard to meet the endless needs of demanding friends. She was exhausted, anxious, and suffered migraines, and she was at a total loss of what to do. Jean was shocked when I told her she had been abused. This is part of the trance of abuse—many victims believe the justifications given for the abuse. Like Jean, often, they don't know they are being abused; they're just trying to survive and figure out how to please the abuser or get out of their way. Jean had no idea that her poor self-image, subservience to exploitative and abusive people, her helplessness to protect herself, and her anxiety attacks were all symptoms of the abuse she had sustained and not flaws that justified the beatings. Jean was on the road to recovery when she discovered the precious little girl in her who was not to blame for the abuse. This is what good therapy does. It makes it safe to explore what happened to us and to uncover the negative, limiting, and untrue beliefs about ourselves—projected onto us by others—that have shaped our coping mechanisms and our sense of self in harmful ways.

This was the work that Jean did. I asked her, "When was the first time you remember feeling fear?" And suddenly, Jean was back at age five, being beaten for having cried when she wasn't allowed to wear a new dress to school. From there, she continued to peel back the layers of shame and unworthiness she had absorbed when her normal child impulses were shamed and punished. Watching her find the little girl in her who only wanted to be loved and accepted and seeing her take one step at a time to protect that part of herself in the present was like watching a little flower open, one petal at a time. It was not easy for Jean, and it was slow going. It had been ingrained in her that the only way she could hope to gain approval or acceptance was to give others whatever they wanted. We worked together for over two years.

Jean stopped sending her father money early on, but it was much harder for her to pull back from exploitive "friends." She was single and had time to spare. She had many professional skills others wanted to make use of, and she was desperate not to lose the connections she had made. We talked about how she could deal with the challenges of her friends' requests and maintain a balance between what felt like appropriate helping, exploitation, and her difficulty saying no to something she really didn't want to do. Slowly, Jean learned to take care of herself in all the ways she had not been taken care of. She was lifting the veil of blame, and her anxiety decreased. I won't pretend there was a quick fix for Jean, at least not one I knew how to provide. The conditioning of years and years of brutal abuse and being forced to serve others at her own expense was not easily undone. It took practice, support, reassurance, and a safe place to process how difficult it was to make changes and advocate for herself. And it also took having a welcoming place to celebrate her successes.

We, here in America, have been conditioned to believe there are people who deserve our judgment and terrible treatment, that poor people are lazy, immigrants are thugs, or LGBQT are sinful. Blaming the victims of nationally perpetrated abuse is so widespread that, like Jean, we don't always know that the cruelty we inflict as a nation is not justified. *No* cruelty is justified. Justification of cruelty is a symptom of a disturbed state of mind. As a nation, we want now to identify the trances of abuse we have been living in—the stories about ourselves and others that we don't always question—that define whole segments of the population as deserving of abuse the way Jean's father portrayed her to herself and her siblings.

Symptoms of Abuse are Not Character Flaws

In 2017, BU Today reported that Ben Carson, then head of the Department of Housing and Urban Development, went on record rejecting the possibility that individuals become poor because of national conditions like diminishing middle-class jobs and wages or the fact that women are paid less than men for the same work, or that this country uses mass incarceration to combat social problems. Carson asserted that poverty is the result of a bad "state of mind," stating, "You take somebody with the right mindset, you can take everything from them and put them on the street, and I guarantee, in a little while, they'll be right back up there . . . You take somebody with the wrong mindset, you can give them everything in the world—they'll work their way right back down to the bottom."[21] This is called the moral construction of poverty: the idea that people are poor because they are lazy, irresponsible, don't want to work, are promiscuous or criminals, or lack intelligence. The article went on to say that Carson's views completely discounted the social structures within which individuals are struggling to make a living. In other words, a high-ranking government official was asserting that the national family has no responsibility for the suffering created by the policies and structures it creates and no responsibility to fix them. This view proposes that people who thrive and succeed in life are morally correct and those who don't are morally deficient, and that victims of a skewed economy are solely to blame for their poverty. One abuser can poison a whole family or community against his targeted victim. One person in a position of national power and authority can promote justifications for abuse and neglect to a whole population. This is how we blame our victims as a country. And we must know this is happening to us.

And the field of psychology tells us that this view of people is simply not the truth. It is, in fact, a sign that the victimizer is not mentally well. He has lost his connection to his fellow human beings. He cannot feel their pain, and this severe lack of empathy makes it possible for him to believe that our larger family systems have no responsibility for the plight of the most hurting individuals. This inability to acknowledge any shared responsibility for the pain of those victimized is a characteristic of abusers, and it is contributing to the mass mental illness plaguing our country.

What Ben Carson's belief illustrates is how easy it is for abusers to blame their victims for both the abuse and their symptoms. We do not blame someone for screaming in pain for a rupturing appendix. We do not blame a stroke victim for being unable to speak clearly. We do our best to help and accommodate them, if not heal them, whenever possible. Yet, for the worst injury and harm we do to one another, abusive people and institutions blame and judge their victims for the ways they express their pain, whether it is the parent who hits their child because he won't stop crying (after they hit the child) or a social and political order that judges the poor as morally deficient, lazy, or "takers," as Carson's point of view illustrates.

There are many symptoms of abuse that are commonly considered "character flaws"—signs of inferiority, sin, ignorance, or perversity—when they should be understood as the expected outcome of ill-treatment at human hands. **These symptoms are normal responses to terribly abnormal and disturbed treatment by other human beings.** Societally, we are slow to make the connection between the degree to which many people are suffering and how symptomatic so many of us have become. As a result, not only do abusers blame their victims, but as a society, we often join in, justifying abuse and blaming victims for their symptoms as well. We know in our psychotherapy offices that the way parents treat their children has everything to do with their children's mental and emotional health, their behaviors, and their ability to function constructively in the world—or not. We learn how to treat ourselves and others from the people in charge. When those in positions of power and influence in our country blame, shame, and continue to target the most vulnerable among us, many of us will unthinkingly absorb this mindset and imitate their beliefs and behaviors.

Victims Believe the Justifications for Their Abuse

Another glaring example of abuse at the national level is that, to this day, the Equal Rights Amendment has not been passed in America. It is legal for employers to pay women less than men for the same work. Many women have protested, but at the same time, other women have been conditioned to believe this injustice is justified, like Jean, who had no idea she was being abused until she heard it from me. My client Liana was a hardworking manager in a small company who had been brought up in a family where men had the last word. She told me it was understandable that she earned less than men in similar positions because women leave work to give birth and are really supposed to be at home with their children. I could not even find the logic in what she said, but the belief that she was not worthy of fair treatment was so deeply internalized that she did not question it. Shocked as I was, I had to wonder how many women still don't believe they are equal to men and, therefore, don't believe they are entitled to equal pay for equal work or other just treatment under the law. And how many more women might there be who do recognize the injustice but feel powerless to do anything about it?

The many ways we have politically and socially blamed victims in America and the ways victims have internalized blame and judgment and become symptomatic are too big to fully cover here. **What we need to remember is that there is no justification for abusing others. It is the abusers' willingness to abuse that leads to their actions, not any behavior or characteristic of their victims.** And it is just as important to remember that abusers are also part of a cycle of abuse, which I will walk you through in more detail as we proceed. It is the perpetrator/victim cycle that needs to be understood and interrupted. Otherwise, we find ourselves right back in the cycle itself, which is all about blame. The evolutionary goal of examining the dynamics of abuse is to get outside the cycle altogether to help us all heal. For now, let's continue taking the cycle apart.

Cries of Pain Are a Normal Response to Violation

It is normal to cry out when being hurt, but that response is also punished by abusers. "Stop crying, or I'll hurt you worse" is not an uncommon threat made to a child who is being molested or beaten. Or they are shamed for being a crybaby—"I didn't hit you that hard." Many learn to stifle their cries because retribution is implied. My client Elisabeth's rebellious older sister was repeatedly beaten by her father. As Elisabeth lay in bed listening to her sister scream, she decided in her seven-year-old mind that she would be "good." She told me she was terrified for her sister, and it took everything not to cry out herself while her sister was being beaten. She learned to stifle what would have been a normal response to her sister's screams. Though she was not the target of her father's rage, Elisabeth knew that if she made any sound of distress or protest, the abuse would come down on her as well. Nor did she ask her mother for help. Elisabeth later discovered that her mother had tried to stop her father only once; the rage he directed at her turned into a fist in her face. Elisabeth had come to therapy because she had difficulty accessing her feelings. She didn't cry, even when her daughter was in an accident; she felt the pain and tears, but they were locked inside her terrified little girl self, who believed that the expression of any upset put her in danger. Like many clients whose symptoms can be traced back to abuse and other injuries to love and belonging in childhood, the work involved visualizing her child self in a safe place and allowing her to express her fears and cry her tears. Toward the end of our work together, Elisabeth started a relationship with a man who was emotionally available and helped her open up even more. What we must know is that the pain and the cries do not go away; they typically create more symptoms, the most glaring of which I will explore with you in the next section of this chapter.

It is normal to cry when beaten. It is a predictable reaction to become resigned when you can't get a job because of the color of your skin. It is normal to try to run or fight back when you are attacked. These are normal responses to the abnormal, abusive conditions so many of us are confronted with, but abusers respond to these normal expressions of self-defense as if the victim is the one in the wrong. Abusive institutions and governments employ the same tactics, making it clear that the cries of those they have hurt and the cries of those who try to defend them will not be heard and will be punished for all to see. They not only threaten opposition voices and truth-tellers, but they publicly discredit and shame them or refuse them the right to be heard. We can look at what happened to Christine Blasey Ford, who risked her life and her reputation to speak her truth about the sexual assault she endured as a young girl from Brett Kavanaugh when he was nominated for Supreme Court Justice. In an article published by ABC News that recounted her public testimony, Blasey Ford talked about the panic and anxiety that still plagued her when she remembered the sexual assault by Kavanaugh and that she had eventually worked on it in therapy and told friends.[22] Yet, as reported by Politico, her trauma and her voice were discounted at the highest reaches of government. "The FBI's investigation into Dr. Christine Blasey Ford's serious allegations about Justice Brett M. Kavanaugh's sexual misconduct was a sham and a major institutional failure . . . Not only did the FBI refuse to interview Dr. Ford or the corroborators listed in our letter to FBI Director Wray, but it failed to act on the over forty-five hundred tips it received about then-nominee Kavanaugh."[23] Instead, the information was given to the White House, and supporters of Kavanaugh falsely claimed that the FBI found no wrongdoing. NPR reported that Blasey Ford felt so unsafe she and her family moved four times. She had to hire her own security, could not go back to her job as a professor, and her own words were,

"My family and I have been the target of constant harassment and death threats."[24] In going public with sexual abuse, Blasey Ford experienced all three of the most devastating responses to her cries. She was demeaned, threatened with assault, and ultimately ignored. Yet I want to point out that none of that stopped her. She called out abuse for her own healing and for the good of the collective of women of America. In the healthiest parts of our population, she was applauded for her bravery.

Abusive governments use many different tactics to threaten and punish victims and their advocates. The last thing an abuser wants is to be held accountable. Therefore, silencing cries of pain and outrage is a first line of defense for abusers; this is an *abnormal* response to a *normal* reaction or symptom of violation. And it models for the country that it is not only dangerous to speak out but that the possibility of being heard will be lost in an onslaught of shame and blame, if not actual assault. George Floyd was an unarmed Black man who was murdered by a policeman in full view of the public. This was an act of deliberate police brutality. A healthy response would be pain and anger and a desire not only for justice for the policeman responsible but for an in-depth overhaul of police practices so that such murders would cease. Pain and outrage were indeed what many Americans felt, and they took to the streets to call out racism and abuse. The response? Tear gas was used on peaceful protesters, and there were mass arrests of demonstrators who were practicing their First Amendment rights. The ACLU reported that "Officers have lined city streets armed with rubber bullets and teargas across the country, and President Trump has endorsed sending in the military, encouraging governors and mayors to use 'overwhelming force' and 'domination.'"[25] This is deliberate abuse of those who are calling out abuse of power! And it sends a message to the Family of America that it is dangerous to have the most normal response to abuse imaginable—pain and protest! We must know that this is happening to untold numbers of Americans today who are terrified to voice their most normal reactions of outrage out of fear of political retribution, police brutality, and public humiliation and alienation.

And still, there is good news, I tell America. *The very good news is that even so, many brave Americans risk life and limb, like Christine Blasey Ford, to speak out anyway. Thousands march in the streets for justice regardless of teargas and rubber bullets.*

Yes, she says, *We can summon amazing courage in the face of overwhelming threats. This is one of our most precious natural resources that we can tap into to steer us to safety.* Her torch may not yet be shining, but her face is lit up.

Another brave American is Bandy Lee, Ph.D., a forensic psychiatrist, who brought together a group of mental health professionals to assess Donald Trump's publicly demonstrated behaviors and rhetoric that she believed, from years of professional experience, pose a real and present threat to America. This is a mental health professional who dared to warn us of mental illness invading the highest reaches of government. She spoke out from a deeply thought-out sense of obligation to warn the public of the dangers posed by Donald Trump's mental condition. She received enormous press until she was shut down by the American Psychiatric Association. And she lost her position at Yale University. Yet she has not given up or stopped sending her message that we are all in danger from malignant narcissists—mentally ill people—in positions of power. She went on to publish a second edition of her book, *The Dangerous Case of Donald Trump: 37 Psychiatrists and Mental Health Experts Assess a President*, in which the seriousness of the former president's mental condition is detailed by experts in the field of mental health.

Some of the most famous martyrs—Jesus, Martin Luther King, and Gandhi were exactly these voices calling out hatred, discrimination, and oppression. They were all advocates of brotherly love and non-violence, *and* they were all murdered. Blasey Ford was trying to save our country from placing a man who had sexually assaulted her in our highest court.

Dr. Bandy Lee was trying to save our country from being run by people who are severely mentally ill. And instead of their warnings being heard, like we would hope to listen to a doctor if we were told we needed surgery or we would die, instead, we persecute the doctor!

We are a strange species. We celebrate our martyrs, mourn their deaths, and create holidays in their names, but we have not yet sat down together and asked ourselves why people must be killed before we can venerate them. What would our lives be like if we had celebrated them and heeded their calls for love, peace, and justice while they were living?

America looks at me intently.

How did we get this way? She asks. *I have been a beacon of hope and salvation for so many people. And yet, we have committed many of the same injustices that the multitudes I welcomed suffered in the countries they fled. Even so, it is also testimony to the strength and perseverance of the American people that many speak out and have not been silenced despite the threats and the attacks. No more martyrs,* she says. *No more killing the messenger. You and I will keep talking, and we will be heard.*

America takes a deep breath, and we continue.

Symptoms of Abuse

The full range of possible symptoms of abuse is too great to go into in detail here (and they have been widely covered in other literature), but they include depression, anxiety, addiction, obsessions, and other mood and behavior disorders, as well as outright violence toward self and others. I want to focus on the outcomes that I believe are most critical to our survival as a country and as a species today. I have selected the top tier of symptoms that I believe put us at the most immediate risk.

Learned Helplessness

When we feel threatened, our alarm bells are supposed to go off immediately. As animals, we know instinctively what to do when a predator is chasing us. Our natural instincts are to fight, flee, or freeze, and we assess the best option without a moment's hesitation. But when our predator is another human being, and particularly one we live with and depend on, instinct alone is often not enough. A child at the mercy of an abusive adult cannot generally fight back or run away with any hope of success, try as they might, though many do try. The other commonly recognized option is to freeze. In the wild, some animals will freeze—hold their breath and not move a muscle—and wait for danger to pass. But when a person lives with an abuser, danger does not pass. This applies both to an individual in an abusive household and to masses of people living within abusive institutions and under threatening governments. Most of us here in America cannot flee either our homes or our country. We have no place to go, or we depend for our existence on those who abuse us.

The dynamics of what holds us in abusive family systems are complex and multi-faceted, and *while I cannot describe them all,* I tell America, *I want to tell you about some of the most damaging adaptations that thousands upon thousands of children and adults are making just to survive.*

When someone smaller or less powerful than the abuser is overpowered and cannot get away or is threatened with terrible consequences for resisting or telling anyone, the next best option is to freeze. This means at some point, they give up. It might be brutal assault that immobilizes them or just a look, eyes filled with hatred, rage, blank indifference, or even pleasure at the pain being inflicted that makes the throat close, the body go limp, the heart seal off, and the mind disappear into a black hole of forgetting where alarm bells no longer sound, where the impulse to fight or flee does not even reach consciousness. In clinical terms, this is called *learned helplessness*, and it manifests on a continuum, from freezing all the way to full-blown dissociation. But we will focus on freezing. We learn that the best way to survive the onslaught is to be helpless. The sad aftermath is that for many victims of abuse, learned helplessness does not go away after the violence has ended (if the violence even ends). It becomes a coping mechanism that is imprinted into the subconscious. **We have learned that it is useless to try to protect ourselves and/or others, so we don't try, as the following two examples illustrate.**

For many who have learned to be helpless, the word NO has been erased from our vocabulary, and access to our natural instinct to say no has been erased as well. My client Mallory's memories of sexual abuse by her mother dated back to when she was three. She then described to me an incident that had occurred not long before I met her. She was sitting alone under a tree in a crowded park when a man approached her. He started what at first appeared to be a friendly conversation but quickly began to tell her what he wanted to do to her sexually. He locked eyes with her, and she froze. She told me she didn't have the thought to get up and walk away or call for help. She froze like a butterfly pinned to a board—until the moment he described a sadistic fantasy that was so violent that something inside her snapped. She woke up out of the trance of her twenty-two years and ran . . . and ran . . . and ran. All the way to therapy. Looking back on the incident, Mallory was horrified at her helplessness in a situation in which she had both the freedom and the physical power to get away and get help but still could not move. In therapy, Mallory recalled that her mother had pinned her down while abusing her and told her that she wanted it and that she liked it. The helplessness she felt was fixed in her psyche as both a body memory—*I have no choice but to endure*—and an emotional memory of confusion, shame, and paralysis. Mallory's work in therapy was to take that little girl to a place of safety now and begin to empower her adult self to advocate for her safety and well-being in the context of her present-day relationships.

For many people, the dynamic of learned helplessness extends to those they love and care for as well. How many times have we heard the story of the mother who stood by and did nothing while her husband or boyfriend beat one of her children? Too many times. How do we imagine anyone could fail to act on that most basic instinct to protect their young?

The good news is that we now know *a lot* about what causes that. We know that that mother most often is a victim of childhood and/or spousal abuse herself. She has already internalized that trying to protect herself or anyone else is futile, and the freezing mechanism kicks in without her conscious consent or control.

My client Rena hid behind the couch when her ex-husband came to her house threatening her with a gun when he heard she had a new boyfriend. Her children ran to the neighbors for help, but when the police arrived, Rena downplayed the incident and refused to press charges. Rena's mother had continually protected Rena's violent, alcoholic father. Rena *learned* to protect abusers and become powerless in the face of assault. She had come to therapy because her son was having nightmares and didn't want to see his father, who still had partial custody, yet Rena felt powerless to get legal help for herself and her child. Was she a bad mother? Many would say yes. She was not protecting her son or herself. But if we are going to help Rena and all those like Rena out there, **we must know that her powerlessness is a *symptom* and not a *cause*. Unaddressed symptoms then become causes of further dysfunction and pain.**

As I watched Rena walk the tightrope between her impulse to protect and her fear of doing so, I wanted so badly to urge her on—get a restraining order, call child protective services, go back to family court to renegotiate custody. While I strongly encouraged her to do all these things, I had to walk a fine line myself between advocating for what I believed needed to happen on the one hand and helping Rena heal the child frozen in fear within her so she could act on her own and her child's behalf. My job was to help Rena work through what disempowered her early on, support her to find appropriate power in the present, and not punish or shame her for the ways she had not been able to generate it on her own.

In exactly the same way, there are thousands upon thousands of working poor in this country who cannot make ends meet with the low wages they receive, cannot afford adequate education to help them qualify for better jobs, or repeatedly do not get hired in the first place because of the color of their skin or the religious garb they wear. They may rely on public assistance for food and housing, or they turn to crime, or, feeling alienated and powerless in a culture that continues to label them inferior, lazy, and entitled, they have given up altogether. Unable to fight or flee, they appear helpless in a culture that has pinned them down economically and then blames them for their inability to succeed.

For our purposes, we want to understand that economic abuse and neglect are just as much abuse as physical violence and sexual assault. Freezing and feeling hopeless and powerless in the face of enormous economic inequality in America are predictable outcomes. According to the 2022 US Census, 12.8% of Americans were living in poverty, 16.9% of them children under the age of eighteen, with variations from state to state. In some states, poverty affects as many as 27.7% of children.[26] ATD Fourth World reports that 37.2 million people live in poverty in the US today, 11.6 million of them children.[27] While it is not within the scope of this book to explore all the causes of poverty in America, it is sobering to understand how enormous income inequality is here and how profound its effect is on millions of people. In an article in Invisible People in January 2021 entitled "Wealth Inequality Gap is Leading to More Homelessness," it was reported that compensation for CEOs is 278 times greater than it is for workers.[28] In speaking about present-day income inequality, David Lazarus, a business columnist for the *Los Angeles Times*, in 2019 stated that the trickle-down theory of economics absolutely did not bring more jobs, improved salaries, or better conditions to millions of Americans. The article stated that while CEOs saved money, they didn't share profits with the lowest-paid workers. Over the last forty years, income inequality has only increased, and so has homelessness. Yet policies supporting a free market continue to be embraced. "And when unregulated capitalism doesn't work, people on the brink of poverty and homelessness are left with little options."[29] This is economic abuse and neglect on a national level, with the poor and the homeless too often being blamed for the helplessness they experience to improve their circumstances.

Any person who has suffered from learned helplessness can tell you that there is almost nothing worse than feeling completely powerless in the face of harm from other people. If not turned outward (which we will discuss later), the pain is often turned against the self—*I'm weak, I'm worthless, I don't deserve better*. Masses of people in America feel helpless in the face of corporate greed and cruel economic policies that allow many of the wealthiest to evade taxes while the middle classes and the poor carry a disproportionate share of the burden. The Institute of Taxation and Economic Policy reported that approximately fifty-five of the largest corporations in the United States did not pay federal corporate income taxes in the 2021 tax season, and this is a pattern that has been repeated for decades. "The tax-avoiding companies represent various industries and collectively enjoyed almost $40.5 billion in US pretax income in 2020, according to their annual financial reports . . . they received $3.5 billion in tax rebates. Their total corporate tax breaks for 2020, including $8.5 billion in tax avoidance and $3.5 billion in rebates, comes to $12 billion."[30]

I, myself, have felt powerless in the face of such economic injustice. As a self-employed single mother of three, for many years, I paid approximately one-third of my income in taxes while I knew there were large corporations paying nothing. **I will repeat here that in a healthy family, everyone is fed, clothed, and housed as well as humanly possible.** No one is taken advantage of, treated unfairly, left out in the cold, or deemed unworthy of being cared for. Yes, national economic policy is different from a single family managing a budget. There will likely always be great differences in our income-earning abilities and in our paychecks. Understood. But when some of the largest corporations pay no income taxes and receive billions in rebates while many of the working poor cannot pay their rent or feed their families on the barest minimum salaries, we must know that something is terribly wrong in the Family of America. We must ask why so many at the bottom of the economic pecking order feel helpless, and instead of blaming them, as Ben Carson did, look at the national family system that renders them more and more powerless.

Discrimination against marginalized communities in the workplace and the justice system and the new wave of voter suppression also leave many Americans feeling powerless. **We are learning to be helpless as whole segments of society in response to the abuse of power by our institutions and by elected officials who have been entrusted to be public servants.** This is exactly what happens to individuals when they are abused in their own homes by those who are supposed to be caring for and protecting them.

Witnesses Also Suffer from Learned Helplessness

Learned helplessness is not confined to obvious victims of abuse and injustice. Many who would consider themselves bystanders also feel helpless. It is terribly upsetting when a relative does not report abuse in a family or a neighbor pretends not to hear a spouse's or child's screams. But what we must know is that, as a nation, we are witnessing flagrant and violent instances of abuse that are beyond the reach of most of us. We hear that poisoned water was knowingly pumped into the homes of the poor in Flint, Michigan, or that defenseless Black people like Briana Taylor and George Floyd were murdered by police, and we have no personal power to intervene. We might have given up hope that a letter to our representatives or vote at the polls would do any good. How many of us fear that what we say on our iPhones or send in a text to a friend is being listened to by "security" forces within our own government? I feel fear writing these words! Is Big Brother watching me? In trying to warn my fellow Americans that the dynamics of abuse in this country have the very real potential to take us all out, am I putting myself at risk?

America sighs again and speaks softly. *What you're saying could be overwhelming to many people,* she tells me. *But I'm trying to remember what you said at the start—that the Hope for Our Country lies in getting the most accurate diagnosis. We cannot treat something if we don't know its causes.*

She sits up straighter now and looks at me more expectantly. I see her hand, perhaps involuntarily, holding her torch a little tighter.

My purpose is not to overwhelm you, I say. America looks so beautiful to me in that moment; I don't want to hurt her. *I hope you know my goal is only to bring into the light of day the psychological dynamics of abuse on all levels so we can heal.*

This is a necessary part of the best therapy—not easy, but necessary. By fearlessly looking at cause and effect, at patterns of conditioning and reaction, we become less and less of a mystery to ourselves, and we begin to understand how we got here, what keeps us here, and, most importantly, what dynamics in human relations need to change in order to defuse the abuse of power.

What I want to explore with you as we proceed, I tell America, *is that the learned helplessness now being imposed on whole segments of society creates a danger to us all.*

In all my years as a psychotherapist, it was not until the lead-up to the 2016 election that I ever had clients come to therapy talking about how traumatized they felt by national politics. An overwhelming number of the people I worked with were suffering anxiety, sleeplessness, and terror over what they were witnessing as a sharp turn to violent rhetoric in the presidential campaign. They reported feeling overwhelming powerlessness at witnessing what felt to them like the destruction of their country and felt they had no way to help stop it. Even those who took action—volunteered with voter registration or wrote to their congress members or contributed to campaign funds of the candidates they felt were a better bet for our mutual safety—even they suffered in proportion to how much they felt their actions were no more than a drop in the ocean as far as their potential effectiveness might be.

And never before in all my years as a therapist have clients used their sessions to talk of their fears that the human race will not survive this dramatic shift toward violence and repression in our nation and around the world. Learned helplessness on the collective level now manifests in everyday statements like, "Well, I guess we're just not going to make it. The earth will be better off without us . . . ."

At the very same time, the sheer feeling of threat has awakened many more people to action, to speak out, to protest, and to realize, perhaps as never before, that we all can have a part to play regardless of our perceived personal reach. Like Mallory, we are waking up from a deep trance of paralysis and the severity of the injuries to our collective mental health that have produced it and running for help.

But let's continue now to look at the second-most common outcome for those who cannot escape abuse.

Identification With the Aggressor

We cannot be hurt by other people without feeling angry. We may not express that anger outwardly, but even if it is inaccessible consciousness, somewhere deep inside, there is a "No, don't do that! Stop!" that wasn't heard, wasn't effective, or never got expressed. The resulting anger (which contains hurt, pain, and powerlessness) is either repressed or explodes, but it doesn't go away. The two most recognizable forms it takes are helplessness and aggression. Aggression and helplessness are two sides of the coin of abuse symptoms.

Those who turn their anger outward as aggression often become bullies—all on a continuum from being mean to siblings or too rough with pets to becoming rapists and murderers. In psychological language, we say they have identified with the aggressor. They, too, are reflecting on what they have learned from abusers who lash out when they can't deal with frustration, conflict, and opposition. Unlike those who have internalized feelings of helplessness, people who identify with the aggressor cannot tolerate feelings of vulnerability and powerlessness. They cope by becoming over-empowered in socially maladaptive ways that mirror the abusive behaviors they have witnessed. They are likely to be intolerant of or enraged by the vulnerability they perceive in others, putting them at great risk for abusing partners and children.

Jerry and his wife, Adele, both in their late forties, came to me for couples counseling. Jerry was a librarian who did yoga regularly, but he was also a rager. His explosions terrified Adele, and she was on the brink of asking for a divorce. The last straw for Adele was an incident in which Jerry smashed a window in Adele's car in a fit of rage. Adele gave him an ultimatum—go to therapy, or she was moving out. In our session, Jerry looked at me petulantly at first, but when he finally opened up about his childhood, he told Adele and me that his older brother had bullied him for years—taunting him at home when their parents were at work and at school as well. Jerry's father was also exceedingly stern and physically punishing. Jerry knew no other way to survive than to be tough. He married Adele because she was soft-spoken and emotional, but he could not meet her there. The more she wanted tenderness from him, the more inadequate he felt. He only knew one way to cope with conflict and feelings of inadequacy, and that was to get angry and bullying, just as his father and brother had been. At first, I wasn't sure I wanted to work with Jerry. In one of our early meetings, he exploded at both me and Adele. Though he agreed to restrain himself for the rest of that session, I wondered if I would be able to get through his wall of defense. I'm not a fan of being raged at, but I knew that was not the point. The point was that I needed to model for both Jerry and Adele a way to address verbal violence that was both powerful and limit-setting but not shaming or blaming. I'm pretty sure I stumbled through it, but I went for the pain beneath Jerry's anger, and he surprised both Adele and me. He did some very deep inner work, uncovered the rage the little boy in him had buried for years, and cried the tears his inner child had not felt safe to cry. Having released the worst of the pain, he learned to control his rage and was eventually able to express more tender feelings for Adele.

Was Jerry a terrible man? His behavior certainly was reprehensible, and it needed to stop, both because he was abusing his wife and losing her but also because he was hurting himself as well. By driving Adele away, he was re-creating the same abandonment that had tormented him as a little boy. While his yoga practice sometimes helped Jerry calm down, it did not heal the deep wounds of early abuse. He was a mystery to himself—he didn't know why he was so rageful or why he couldn't stop it. And until he came to therapy, the shame he felt about his behavior toward Adele only produced more anger and aggression. The answer that therapy held for Jerry was to help him work with the little boy inside who felt so powerless to get the love and care he desperately wanted from his father and brother. It was not an easy road for Jerry. He wanted to blame Adele for his anger, but the more he worked with his own abuse, the more he was able to hear, without so much defensiveness, the terrible impact he was having on her. He was able to hear *her pain* rather than be solely focused on his own. He gradually felt safer to be vulnerable with her and allow her to be vulnerable with him. Was it perfect? No, Jerry had a lot to work through, but once he found the victim inside himself and could feel empathy for what he had gone through in his childhood, he had a place to come back to when he felt like he was losing it. The little boy victim in Jerry wanted only to love and be loved; the abuser in him wanted to hurt others. The challenge was to both stop the abuser and help heal his younger self.

Addressing Violence without Violence

I will go into this issue in greater length in the closing chapters of the book, but it may serve as a helpful lead-up to highlight that Adele made the best call when she told Jerry to get help or she would leave him. He needed to hit a limit to rein himself in, and fortunately for them both, he did his very best to control himself and work with the source of his anger, and he had a partner who was willing to stand by him. The challenge for us here in America is similar to the one Jerry and Adele faced—to understand as much as possible the roots of violence and have empathy for the pain inside many of the most violent among us while *we hold them accountable* for what they have done *and* stop them from continuing to hurt others. We need to meet this challenge with the best skills for healing human relations as a first line of defense—without shame and retaliation and with legal restraint as a last (though sometimes necessary) resort.

Hard as it may be to take in, as much as we may still want to make the abuser wrong and even hate the abuser (as distinct from holding the abuser accountable), whether it is the parent who broke their child's arm or the governing body that enslaved a race, as much as we may still feel rage at the offenses abusers have committed and the suffering they have caused, we must know that the only way to get out of the closed loop of victim and perpetrator is to **end violence without violence. The only way we can stop the cycle of repeated and intensified Low-Tech Human Relations in our homes, communities, and in the highest reaches of government is to hold ourselves and all others accountable, employ appropriate restraint when necessary, and commit to healing everyone—abused and abuser alike.**

It is difficult to remember this when I hear that another Black person is killed by police at a "routine" traffic stop or a twelve-year-old rape victim is denied the right to terminate her pregnancy. It is difficult to think about the victims inside the people who inflict so much pain on others and not succumb to outrage and hatred myself. I remind myself that abusers are mentally ill, and while there are many who need to be restrained because they are a threat to others, if we really don't want to be at the mercy of mentally ill people who believe in violence and who cannot feel empathy for others, we must address *the conditions furthering abuse* in our families and in our governing institutions that keep producing more and more people who identify with the aggressor. To do this, one of the most important things we need to know is that **inside the perpetrator is very likely a victim who never got help.** Treating abusers with the same aggression that produced them in the first place will never work to resolve the violence that plagues us. It would be like trying to cure someone of alcoholism by giving them copious amounts of alcohol.

Abuser and Victim Are Drawn to Each Other

To reiterate, unchecked abuse produces more and more people who either become helpless and easily controlled or aggressive and cruel. Those who become aggressive then target those who are more easily controlled, and those who have learned to become helpless are often easy prey for abusers because they instinctively freeze, as Mallory did with the man in the park. On the micro level, it is well known, for example, that molesters have a keen sense for spotting children who have already learned to be submissive and helpless. And in my experience over many years, almost without exception, I found that clients who had an abusive mother also had a very passive father and vice versa. The dynamic of dominance and submission both characterized the family dynamic and role-modeled it for the children. On an unconscious level, the moth-to-flame dynamic of attraction between aggressor and submitter gets passed down from one generation to another. This is how abuse and the climate of widespread mental illness it generates accelerate on the level of the individual family, what I am calling Low-Tech Human Relations on the micro level. This has profound implications for our national mental health, well-being, and ultimate safety, as I will continue to explore with you.

In addition, people who have been overpowered themselves, regardless of what coping mechanisms they have adopted, are also at risk of idealizing and joining ranks with those they believe are as powerful and as invulnerable to pain as they want to be. They can be attracted to the bully on the playground, join gangs, and abuse positions of power themselves and support others who do so. There are many examples of these dynamics playing out in America today, but let's look at one that has been extremely dangerous for this country in recent history.

Identification with the Aggressor on a National Scale

Although there has not been any concrete evidence to support the claim of a stolen election in 2020, *Meet the Press Blog* reported that as of September 2022, 61% of Republicans still believed Biden did not win the election.[31] And *Newsweek* reported right before the mid-terms in early November 2022 that 40% of Americans still held that belief.[32] At the same time, the *Texas Tribune* article on November 4, 2022, reported that US Representative Dan Crenshaw, a Republican from Houston, stated that members of Congress who challenged the 2020 election admitted out of the public eye that the claims of a stolen election were false. He was quoted as saying, "It was always a lie. The whole thing was always a lie. And it was a lie meant to rile people up."[33]

Lies on this scale are an *abuse* of the American people. Many Americans were conscripted into believing these falsehoods, and thousands acted violently (identification with the aggressor) in support of this abuse of power. The January 6 insurrection is a terrifying outcome of abuse dynamics playing out on the national level. Our Congressmen and women came perilously close to being physically assaulted by an angry mob of thousands! A crowd riled up by falsehood and identifying with an abuse of power cost five people their lives in the insurrection itself and immeasurable damage to our country's belief in the electoral process, as well as widespread attacks on voting rights. By looking at the outcomes of abuse, such as learned helplessness and identification with the aggressor, we have new insight into who the people are who are most susceptible to being enrolled in hatred and violence on a mass scale and who would be most easily overcome by it.

While I do not know all the motivations for those who supported the idea of election fraud in the 2020 presidential election, the fact that this occurred at a high level within the government itself may help us understand the last big outcome of abusive family dynamics that I want to share with you.

The Abuser is Rewarded

Along with an underlying threat that it is dangerous to oppose an abusive person in power, there are often overt rewards for participating in the abuse. What happened to Jean is an example of how this dynamic occurs in an individual family. Jean's siblings were made to hold her down while her father beat her, and he also rewarded them for helping him, especially as Jean grew older. The sisters received presents and privileges Jean did not get, and they eventually joined in the verbal abuse of Jean as well. When Jean came for therapy, her siblings were calling her with the same angry, accusing messages her father was delivering. They had been indoctrinated to believe Jean deserved the abuses hurled at her, and they thus convinced themselves that they were as justified in attacking her as their father was. From little children forced to participate in abuse, they became adults who believed they were justified in abusing. They had been conscripted.

We will never know how many are conscripted into the abuse of power in our country for all the above reasons, but we do know that abuse is widespread in families across America, and many of those who do not find escape and help are easier prey for abuse from high places. **The even sadder news is that to the extent we are drawn into the web of the abuser with rewards, the incentive to protect the abuser's victims can all but disappear.** Many of us ask ourselves how it can be that so many in positions of power have become (historically and in the present) so callous to the pain they are inflicting on others, how people with children they love can become willing to tear other people's children—infants even—from their parents' arms. As we look deeply into the dynamics of abusive family systems mirrored nationally (and, of course, internationally as well), we begin to see what psychology has taught us—that if the victim and perpetrator dynamic is not stopped, and our collective psychology is not addressed as a national issue, the psychological weapons of mass destruction we are outlining here will take us to a place of unfathomable inhumanity, with fewer of us able to resist, and the remorse necessary to pull us back from that ledge will have been systematically destroyed. This does not have to happen! It does not have to be a mystery any longer why such violence and hatred can consume us when we are all born wired for love and connection.

Chapter 5:

VICTIMS, SURVIVORS, AND VICTIMIZERS: UNPACKING THE ROLES OF ABUSE

hope it is beginning to become clear that the ways we are taught to think about human behavior and the language we use to describe it have everything to do with how we perceive and judge ourselves and others and how we react. If a child is rambunctious and not easily reined in, he might be described as lively and spirited and in need of greater structure and direction, or he can be labeled oppositional and disobedient and shamed and punished. Women who wear low-cut clothing and short skirts can be seen as embracing their femininity or labeled loose, provocative, and deserving of assault. Our values affect the language we use, and our language conditions our values and judgments of ourselves and others. Abusers deliberately use language to categorize their victims as evil, inferior, and deserving of abuse and to minimize their responsibility for the harm they inflict. While the subject of psychological conditioning and manipulation is bigger than the scope of this book, there is one specific way that language is manipulated by both individual abusers and abusive cultures alike that deserves particular attention. The word victim suddenly has a negative connotation. It is only since the 1980s here in America that victims, especially victims of sexual assault and abuse, began speaking publicly. Victims had stories to tell. They were talking to therapists and to each other, confronting family members, writing books, and speaking to the press. What had been going on for years behind closed doors was coming into the light of our own individual consciousness and into the light of day.

And just as suddenly, speaking the pain of victimization, naming names, and breaking family and societal rules of silence and the protection of perpetrators—just as suddenly, it was being debunked! The term "false memory syndrome" sprang up like a weed, casting long shadows of doubt and choking out the voices of so many courageous truth-tellers. Mothers didn't want to believe their husbands had molested their daughters. No one wanted to admit anything. As quickly as victims spoke up, they were repudiated or blamed for what happened to them, especially girls and women. *She shouldn't have worn those tight pants. What does she expect if she went home with him?* Men and boys spoke up less often—the shame of male victimization was even more stigmatizing.

Almost as quickly as we let Pandora out of the box, the full force of denial tried to slam it shut. One dictionary definition of the word victim is "a person harmed, injured, or killed as a result of a crime, accident, or other event or action." There is nothing in the definition that states or implies that the person harmed is either weak or is in any way responsible for the harm done to them. Yet we don't often hear the word victim used today that way because, almost overnight, the connotations of whininess and self-pity have been added on like so many leeches, sucking the blood from an already open wound. The word victim now drags behind it the unfortunate connotation of languishing too long in pain, being unwilling to get back up and recover, playing the sympathy card, or not thinking enough positive thoughts.

Today, we don't talk about being victims; we are survivors. We are thrivers. Victim is suddenly an old paradigm. I'm not arguing against reframing ourselves as survivors—absolutely not. The word survivor rightfully heralds the possibility of healing. It tells us trauma doesn't have to destroy us and that we can go on to live even more vibrant lives. We do not want to be defined by what happened to us but by who we are in our essence and what we have made of ourselves. But the positivity inherent in the word survivor can also inadvertently become a terrible disservice. It can urge us to bypass what happened that we have had to survive. **We are surviving being victimized. We are thriving *after* victimization.** Feeling the pain of what someone (or something) did to us, getting help for as long as we need to work our way out of that abyss is not "playing the victim." It is not an unwillingness to see the light. It is, in fact, honoring the truth of our own being. It is honoring the journey of survival, which is a journey, not a word change. We wouldn't say we are surviving a trip to the grocery store. We only use that word if we are surviving something that has the potential to take us out.

I'm not suggesting we *stay* in the mindset of the word victim. I'm saying we must not skip over it. If we cannot use the word victim freely, we cannot feel the full pain of having been hurt by others. If we are only allowed to be survivors, we cannot fully call out perpetration. And if we cannot fully call out perpetration, we cannot fully hold others (or ourselves, if it is us) accountable. Our subtle and not-so-subtle use of language reflects and alters our self-perception and our experience, and it serves perpetrators to malign the word victim and those who dare to say they have been hurt. It casts victims as weak and whining, as seen in Tucker Carlson's mockery of Alexandria-Ocasio-Cortez when she went public about being sexually harassed on the steps of the Capitol. This behavior diverts responsibility away from the abuser and puts it on the victim, which is a tactic we described earlier that abusers employ to deflect responsibility away from themselves.

The beauty of psychotherapy and all true healing work is that it both honors and listens to the victim in us while it sees and empowers the survivor in us.

I love this, America says. *What you're saying gives me hope that we can recognize the abuses we heap on our victims simply by the terrible ways we talk about them. You make it so clear that we need to get beyond labels, beyond the more disguised levels of name-calling, and look deeply into the ways language alone can be used to hurt or heal.*

Yes, exactly, I say. *And that work around language needs to extend to the victimizer as well.*

Victim and Victimizer are Two Sides of a Coin: Both are Victims

What is evolutionary and revolutionary for our understanding is that the helplessness and the aggression resulting from abuse have deep roots in feelings of powerlessness. Neither coping mechanism heals the trauma of being rendered utterly powerless by someone who hurts us. Though these two coping mechanisms look entirely different, they are two sides of the same coin, two different ways the psyche tries to address the same wound. Neither outcome is a character flaw. They are not signs of deficient or defective personalities. They are both symptoms of abuse. The one who becomes aggressive and the one who becomes helpless are both victims. This is our next big *Aha!* It is perhaps easier to see that the person who freezes or who is simply overpowered, even if they resist assault, is a victim. It is harder to see that the ones who identify with the aggressor as a result of abuse and out of fear of their own vulnerability are equally victims. **What we have discovered in psychology is that treating the victim inside all of us is the key to healing.** There are, of course, people so psychologically damaged we don't know how to restore them to safety, and they must be restrained. But there are many more who are not candidates for incarceration. Like Jerry, they are candidates for healing! Or in the case of Rena, who could not protect her children, the healing approach is to understand her as a traumatized woman who needed help to become appropriately empowered and protective rather than condemn her for negligence. The focus that is evolutionary is in understanding how the family or the individual got out on such a precarious ledge in the first place and to bring them back—individual families and the Family of America.

Many people will ask: if we understand that the perpetrator is also a victim, are we supposed to excuse them because they had a bad childhood? While this is an understandable question, we need to look at the issue through a new lens. Nothing presented here is intended to be an excuse for terrible behavior. But if we stay focused on symptoms, in this case, the symptom of identification with the aggressor, we can easily forget the cause. The problem is *abuse* and what results when it is not stopped or treated. Let's look at it this way. If two people contract the same flu, one might have a fever and chills, and another might get a sore throat and a headache. They both got the same germs, but their bodies react differently. We need to know all possible symptoms of the flu to find the best treatment and prevention for the flu itself, no matter how it manifests. The problem we are facing in the epidemic of abuse and mass mental illness associated with it here in America is that we do not yet have a common understanding of the full range of abuse symptoms, which we need if we are going to stop its spread and invest in the best ways to treat it. Prevention ultimately is the cure, and it is based in an understanding and implementation of High-Tech Human Relations on every level of our social structure.

This is a big revelation, America says. *I wonder how many people outside the psychology world have any idea of what you're talking about. Our investment in the belief that some people are good and others are evil and that we must conquer the evil goes back millennia. You're talking about a complete paradigm shift.*

We sit together in silence for a moment as America takes this in.

Chapter 6:

OUR SYMPTOMS ARE A CRY FOR HELP

Sometimes, I imagine I am looking down on earth from far out in space. I see the green and blue glow of our planet lit up by the sun and the misty white clouds circling above this landscape we have been so blessed to inhabit. I think about rainforests and dolphins and the hummingbirds I love to watch in the summertime around my backyard feeders. It is such a beautiful world. Then, I think of us humans, the farmers and teachers, the old people and the babies just being born, clean houses, the homeless, and all the people going hungry while others have more food and more money than they could ever consume. And then I think of a child sold into sex trafficking and the person willing to purchase that child's body, and I think of war, of thousands and millions of people being killed by other people. I can't help but feel we look more than a little cruel from that point of view. I understand that animals kill other animals for food and that we all need to eat from other living kingdoms to stay alive. I understand that it is part of being born into mortal bodies that some creatures die so that others can live. But we humans are the only ones who kill out of hatred, greed, and belief systems that do not allow for alternate views or lifestyles. We are the only ones who purposely abuse and kill our own children and systematically kill millions of our own species. Stepping outside and far above my personal wants and needs of the day, beyond the latest news of who got elected and who didn't and what is the latest threat from climate change—from that removed point of view, it looks very much like the human race is suffering from a serious autoimmune disorder (in which the body attacks itself), but it's not a disease of the body; it's a disease of the heart and mind. It's mental illness. And from far above the fray, it is easier to hear the cries of the wounded above all the noise of politicians and the angry voices of a fired-up mob going after a Black or gay person, a woman, or even someone trying to help.

The hope of everything I do, I tell America, *is that we listen to our own cries, that we recognize them for what they are and are not afraid to act, not frightened into silence, and not provoked into aggression. My hope is that we can learn to hear our own cries the way good parents hear the cries of their children when they are injured, sick, terrified, or under attack.*

To do this, we must learn how to step outside the victim and perpetrator cycle in our own behaviors and attitudes. One of the keys is to understand that the worst symptoms—violent aggression, dangerous passivity, and insidious collusion with abuse, as well as the direct cries of pain of those most targeted and injured—are *all* a Cry for Help!

We know this now without a doubt from our work with families in our individual psychotherapy offices. The most symptomatic among us are those crying the loudest for intervention. The severity of their symptoms, whether it be that they freeze in the face of abuse of their own children or they murder innocent first graders, lets us know something is terribly amiss not only in the individual family but in the Family of America as a whole. Our most disturbed behaviors on all fronts are screaming at us to come to our own rescue. It is the climate of abuse and the mental illness affecting so many of us that keeps us from hearing our own cries or taking them seriously. This is the Terror of the Situation, and once again, psychology holds Hope for Our Country.

Years of doing family therapy has taught me that children like Michelle and Benny are the ones who get the family into therapy. They have no idea they are calling for help for the family, but we therapists do know. We know to look beyond their symptoms to what is not working in the family, and we work with that. **This is the blueprint for *America in Therapy*. We must look beyond the behaviors of the most dysfunctional and disturbed among us, listen to what is causing the pain they are manifesting, and then look at the dynamics of our country that are contributing to their cries.** If warring, neglectful, and abusive parents account for so much childhood pain and troubled behaviors, we must know that these same dynamics on the level of the Family of America are at the root of our collective pain and acting out as well.

All the most problematic children I have worked with (and adults, too, for that matter) were reacting to hostility, violence, abandonment, and deprivation of some kind in their homes and immediate environment. Yet, who was most identified as having the problem? Not the parents but their symptomatic children. In psychotherapeutic terms, we call Michelle, Carol, Justin, and Benny the identified patients. This means that they are identified as the ones having the problem. A focus on the identified patient keeps us from seeing the underlying family problems when, in fact, they are the ones who show the family pain to the world. Their symptoms are the emotional equivalent of a fever or swelling in the body. We don't get angry at a fever; we look for the cause and the cure. One of the greatest contributions of family systems theory today is that we now know that the most symptomatic family members at every level of society—the addict, the rapist, and the despot—are alerting their own families and the world around them that something is terribly wrong in the human family. Their symptoms are the Cry for Help we all need to hear.

I understand that this is a dramatically new way of seeing and understanding human behavior for many people. We have been conditioned to believe there are simply good and bad people. But using the body analogy, we don't say it is a bad organ if we have cirrhosis of the liver. We know that the whole body has been poisoned with alcohol, and the liver has become symptomatic to tell us to *stop drinking*. This is how we must look at the Family of America if we want to have any hope of safety and survival as a species. When the body of the Family of America is ill, is operating on abuse dynamics, or is being governed by people who are mentally unwell, there will inevitably be people who become symptomatic, like the alcoholic whose liver becomes diseased. The child and spousal abusers, murderers, sex traffickers and producers of child porn, drug dealers and scammers, police who brutalize peaceful protesters, and all those in positions of power who reap great rewards for exploiting, oppressing, and terrorizing others—they are some of our most blatant symptom bearers, the identified patients of America. They are the tip of a huge iceberg of national dysfunction—the part that shows. Our job as a nation is to look at what is underneath, at the increasing hostilities between opposing parties, economic groups, races, religions, and genders that create the troubled family dynamics we are all struggling to adapt to. Our most pressing job as a nation is to commit to resolving these hostilities for the sake of every one of us.

As much pain and horror as the Uvalde shooter inflicted on innocent children, their families, a community, and a nation, one critically important interpretation of his actions that psychology can offer us is that he *also* sounded an alarm (as all mass shooters are doing) that the dangerous state of our collective mental health has us all at risk. The Cry for Help that rang out even with the shooter's own death is to get the Family of America to therapy.

A Cry for Help That Was Heard

I want to tell you there is hope. Kevin was a sixteen-year-old boy I worked with briefly before his family moved away. Kevin lived with his younger brother and mother. He originally came to see me for depression. Kevin had been verbally and physically abused by his father, who, fortunately, he was no longer forced to visit. As we delved into what had happened to him, Kevin revealed to me that he had fantasies of violence that frightened and worried him. I was the only one he had told. He felt powerless and angry, had nightmares of being chased and assaulted, and his overwhelmed psyche compensated by fantasizing that he was the one to inflict pain on others. Kevin was walking the fine line between victim and perpetrator. Fortunately, therapy was available to him, and he had the internal strength to disclose his deepest fears and shame. In our therapy, Kevin visualized the abused little boy in him being rescued and taken to safety, where he could tell his story, cry, vent some of his anger, and be held and comforted by Kevin's teenage self. As he did this, his violent fantasies subsided. Kevin was not a bad person or deranged. He was a terribly hurting young man, and his symptoms were a Cry for Help.

It is the therapist's job to stand outside the victim/perpetrator closed loop of dysfunction and help the victim inside the perpetrator. As I have stated many times in this book, we are not always effective, and there are people we do not identify soon enough or don't yet know how to help. Even more frightening is the fact that there are untold numbers of Kevins out there who will never make it to therapy or get help of any kind. It is terrifying to think of what happens to them and what they are capable of. It is my deepest hope that in writing about the massive Cry for Help of the Family of America (and around the globe), we can all learn—as family members, friends, employers and employees, witnesses and participants, and as fellow citizens—to stand outside the victim/perpetrator dynamic and offer help wherever we can. The first place to begin is by educating ourselves. This is why I share with you, dear reader, everything I have learned about how to do this. In later chapters, I will address the part we can all play in greater detail.

Getting Outside the Tight Web of Abuse

It is up to *all of us* to hear the Cry for Help from the victims and abusers among us and intervene. Those who can step outside the victim and perpetrator dynamic have the best chance of hearing those cries and can, therefore, offer the greatest hope to those still trapped within it. These people are our allies, and we desperately need more of them. They represent the alternative to the plague of violence in America. These are the people we can count on to have empathy for the pain of others and who will actively participate in bringing healing to the rest of us, whether on the scale of a one-to-one in their personal circles or in larger social and political arenas. These are the people we want to be listening to, helping us, and leading us. And we want to know they can be effective without resorting to any of the forceful dynamics of abusers. Whether it is a neighbor or teacher who offers refuge or rescue to an abused child, a community leader or program that creates opportunity and services for the forgotten, or those willing to stand up and speak out to abusive authority and demand justice, our best hope of recovery from the ravages of abuse and neglect is to find other people who are committed to High-Tech Human Relations who want to help.

The good news is that there are many people both in the past and in the present who have done exactly what I am talking about. In an article in *Global Citizen Magazine* about peaceful protests that were effective in overturning abusive policies, this was written about Rosa Parks: "There are times when one person's peaceful actions can bring about more change than anyone can imagine. Rosa Parks' refusal to give up her seat to a white passenger on a bus in Montgomery, Alabama, is one such example."[34] The article described her defiance as a powerful symbol of civil rights that spread the message that everyone deserves equal seats. Her action was so powerful that a year later in, 1956, the US Supreme Court ruled segregation on public buses was unconstitutional. Rosa Parks stood outside the abusive racial policies in the South and showed us another way, simply by sitting in a seat she was not allowed to sit in. She was defiant but not violent. She showed us how we can stand outside an abusive social order, bearing no weapons and no words of hatred, and open the doors to a new social order. I say this knowing full well that a new social order is not yet here, that Black people in America still suffer terrible discrimination and injustice, and that we have a long way to go. But that does not diminish the power and effectiveness of what Rosa Parks did. We can see by the peaceful protests to end police brutality, for economic justice for the 99%, and for women's right to be protected from sexual assault and the right to decide for their own bodies that there are many Americans hearing a multitude of Cries for Help right now and answering the very best they can.

The work of Father Gregory Boyle is a wonderful example of one man hearing the Cry for Help from a terribly reviled population of Americans and showing us how the victim and perpetrator cycle can be interrupted and healed in a very short time with dramatic results—which is the whole point of interrupting the cycle of abuse! In 1986, Father Gregory Boyle became pastor of Dolores Mission Church, the poorest Catholic parish in Los Angeles that had the highest concentration of gang activity. He started out trying to improve the lives of former gang members in East Los Angeles, and his work evolved into Homeboy Industries, the largest gang intervention, rehab, and re-entry program in the world. Every year, Homeboy Industries welcomes thousands of people into their community of love and kinship to transform their lives with job opportunities, mental health services, parenting classes, support for domestic violence, and substance abuse help. In Father Boyle's own words, "We work with the population that nobody desires to work with, and it's a principle of this place that we stand with them." The Homeboy Industries website goes on to state that they work with people who have been left without hope, that the people they serve are not expected to recover quickly, and many don't, but that the impact of what Homeboy Industries offers as hope and opportunities for healing, job training, and community building is clear from each life transformed. As their lives change, they change the lives of their families and communities. The dedication of Homeboy Industries creates "a positive ripple effect not only around the city of Los Angeles but in communities around the world."[35]

An article in The Manual stated it this way: "It's dangerously easy to dehumanize gang members. In reality, joining a gang is often a sign that the person has been badly failed by society. One priest in Los Angeles realized these men and women didn't need 'tough on crime,' they needed hope and opportunity."[36]

For well over thirty years, Father Boyle has responded to this Cry for Help. Rather than passing judgment, he sees human beings in pain who need love, connection, and support, regardless of their past. Law enforcement tactics of suppression and a criminal justice system bent on mass incarceration are the epitome of Low-Tech Human Relations, but these are still the prevailing means to deal with gang violence in America. This approach is based in the belief that the extremes of harsh judgment and punishment are the keys to the cure for crime. Yet Father Boyle's work is an example of High-Tech Human Relations at its best. It is stunning testimony that love and care are what is needed to bring lasting healing to people whose lives have been nearly destroyed by alienation and violence, that people who have grown up with severe abuse and neglect, who have committed crimes and served time in prison, can transform their lives and become loving, contributing members of society. Homeboy Industries has created a tangible experience of home and family for thousands of former gang members for whom the experience of family was once either frightening, dangerous, or non-existent. And with that, there is *hope* for all of us because their children and all those they interact with have the benefit of the hard work of healing they have done to break the cycle of abuse they came from. In Father Boyle's words, "We imagine a world without prisons, and then we try to create that world."[35]

It's never too late to hear our collective Cry for Help. It's not too late for America to pick up the same gauntlet that Rosa Parks, Father Boyle, and so many like them are carrying. There are countless people already working to care for those in need in concrete ways. We may not know their names, and their stories of caring and generosity may not make it to the news, but they are out there, too—the many who have already heard the Cry for Help and are setting up food banks, creating mobile medical services and libraries, showing people in the inner city how to grow their own food, teaching alternative justice to teenagers, funding dance programs for disadvantaged children, and getting out on the playground to help children build compassion for one another and end bullying. The list is endless.

America closes her eyes. She is weeping. *As a country and as a culture, I have been waiting to understand the Cry for Help from my own people for a very long time. And it does not escape me that the very same cry is echoing around the world.*

Chapter 7:

FACING PAIN TO HEAL

Physical pain lets us know we have left the safe zone of our physical existence. We would not know we are dying from appendicitis if we didn't feel pain. It calls us to find the cause and the cure. Emotional pain tells us we have left the safe zone of our emotional existence, which is primarily determined by our relationships with other people. Emotional pain is almost always a signal that something in our relationship world is not working, harmful, threatening, or missing. Why? Because it is primarily in relationship with other people that we experience the most devastating emotional injuries—betrayal, abandonment, injustice, deprivation, and physical, sexual, and emotional assault. **And it is also in relationship that these injuries can be healed. Finding safety means finding safe people.** When we eat good food, we feel great. Contaminated food makes us sick. When we are fed love and connection, our psyches thrive. Hatred and violence make us emotionally ill. This is not rocket science. Emotional illness is caused by a toxic psychological diet in our relationship world. In a word, abuse, as we have defined it, is the toxic emotional environment that is making us emotionally and mentally ill.

The human psyche, as well as the human body, can only stay healthy and survive within a certain safe range of emotional-mental input and output. Instinctively, we tune in to our level of emotional comfort or discomfort all day long without necessarily thinking about it, just like we tune into whether we are hot, tired, or hungry. We assess the signals— our own anxiety, her smirk, his welcoming smile—and we evaluate our level of ease or unease mostly automatically until we are approaching the danger zone. Extremes of hatred, violence, alienation, and injustice, as well as extremes of depression, panic, hopelessness, fear, and rage, are the danger zones. To the extent that we can protect and defend ourselves, get away, get help, and mend the hurt, the pain of these conditions is a useful signal. It warns us to find safety. But when we cannot get away from an abusive family or larger social or political system, when we are blamed and silenced, and when we witness assault and even murder of others and are helpless to intervene, then our pain, which should be a motivator, becomes a source of endless suffering.

Obviously, emotional pain is an unavoidable part of human life. There is often no safe zone we can go to that will simply take away the pain of a divorce, a job loss, an accident, or the death of a loved one. We are all given endless opportunities to learn patience, control our anger, grieve, or get back up after a loss or failure. But how do we learn these things? Most often, we learn them from other people—parents, friends, admired leaders, teachers, and healers. It is in the world of relationships that we learn how to tolerate our distress successfully or not. An empathic response and supportive connection with another person can help ease emotional pain like nothing else. Responses of shame, blame, punishment, and ignoring only increase the pain.

Our Greatest Pain Comes from Failed Human Relations

In all the years I have been a psychotherapist, I have not had one client who could not trace their emotional pain and problems back to deficient, failed, or cruel human relationships. Our most agonizing feelings and the destructive behaviors we suffer from all have their origins in how we were treated or are being treated now by those we are attached to, depend on, and who have the most power over us. Psychotherapy shows us the way out of whatever our most painful conditioning has been because it models what a restorative relationship looks like. In the safety of the therapeutic relationship, we go into our pain to discover what happened to us and what we have been conditioned to believe and do that has hurt us so that we can release that pain and find new ways of being that promote safe, healthy relationships with ourselves and others. In this context, pain is a doorway to healing.

One of the most painful things we can experience if we let ourselves is the pain of acknowledging the things we ourselves have done that have been hurtful to others. Most of us, if we are honest with ourselves, even if we have been terribly abused and that becomes the focus of our work, will see at some point that we, too, have been hurtful to others. We may not have assaulted or killed anyone, but the victim in us is the part that becomes the victimizer. As we explored earlier, inside every perpetrator is a victim. Inside most of us who have been victimized is also a victimizing energy. It may be subtle, or it may be overt. It may be mostly turned on ourselves as self-hatred, self-sabotage, addiction, or other forms of self-harm, or it may come out as sniping at others, betrayals we have committed, or prejudices we have acted on. Or both. It is important to name the worst offenders among us, those who rape, steal and kill, but one of the very best ways to understand them as victims themselves is to feel the pain of acknowledging the victimizer within us. The best psychotherapy makes it safe for us to do both—feel the pain of what hurt us and the pain of acknowledging the hurt we have caused. Both are needed for healing.

Facing Pain Uncovers Buried Treasure

Before we leave this part of our discussion, let's understand one of the most positive and hopeful reasons to face our pain through my client Monica's story. Monica came to therapy for anxiety and depression after her husband left her for another woman. She had a demanding job, two small children, and very little help from her ex. She was overwhelmed, but she kept going day after day. She had no off switch. Monica had a history of sexual abuse that she had never allowed herself to process. It had come up in her first attempt at therapy several years before I met her, but she had quit therapy before diving in. Like so many of us, Monica told herself she should put the past behind her, but the truth was she was afraid that once she started crying, she would never stop. Functioning with a high level of competency and productivity was both how she survived and how she tried to keep unwanted feelings at bay. She dreaded going to bed because the dark feelings would come up, so she kept the TV on until she fell asleep. Monica described the following experience to me.

She was in her late twenties at the time. It was a beautiful sunny day, and she was walking to her mailbox when suddenly, as if from nowhere, as if it were a flash of light itself, she had a deep knowing that her real self was buried deep within and had never come out. It was enormous and beautiful, like the sun above her, but she could see it had been squished down to the size of a pinhead. By the time she came to see me, the pain of abuse in her childhood had burst through into consciousness, and she finally knew that in burying her painful past, she had also buried access to her essential self. She knew there was no way around the pain; she needed to go through it. She worked with the sexual abuse, remembering some very terrifying experiences and, yes, crying the river of tears she had so feared. We talked about how the therapy process helps peel back the layers of hurt, fear, shame, and self-judgment that cover over the essential self that she had experienced bursting through so powerfully when she was younger. I did a process with Monica called EMDR (Eye Movement

Desensitization Reprocessing) in which, through rhythmic stimulation to the two hemispheres of the brain, Monica was able to access thoughts, feelings, sensations, and memories that were not available to her conscious mind. All this material was "reprocessed." This meant, in short, that in constant contact with me as her guide, Monica was able to safely go back into traumatic memories and uncover the most negative beliefs about herself that she had taken on from early abuse. The main negative belief for Monica was that it was unsafe to show her real self in any way, and as a result, she had cut herself off from her emotional life and self-expression. Watching Monica reprocess the abuse, guiding her to visualize taking her little girl self to safety, and reflecting back her innocent essence helped Monica internalize more positive beliefs about herself. Bit by bit, the suffocating layers of abuse lifted, and her buried essence became the radiant center of her life. We worked together intensively for about two years. I was in awe myself as, almost miraculously, Monica became more social, took part in a local play, and eventually remarried. She continues, like all of us, to meet challenges and difficulties, but she can face them with resources and strength she had no access to before.

People often ask why it is necessary to go back through all that pain. Can't we just move on? And what I say is this: If we could just bury our pain and all the negative thoughts, feelings, beliefs, and body sensations that are attached to it, we would, and that would be the end of it. But my experience has shown me that an essential part of who we are gets buried along with our suffering, and it is our deep longing to uncover and reunite with that essential self that brings us to therapy or other help. Good therapy speaks to that essential self and helps uncover it (more on this later).

Revisiting Pain in a Safe Therapeutic Setting is Not Retraumatizing

I want to emphasize that the best psychotherapy honors and facilitates releasing pain as a necessary and *valued* part of the journey of recovery. In a world where we have come to expect instant gratification, a pill for every pain, and high-speed everything, it often seems counter-intuitive that a quick fix is not always a fix at all. Many people believe that uncovering a painful past will retraumatize them. I have found quite the contrary to be true in a safe therapeutic setting. Unprocessed trauma too often festers like an unhealed infection, causing even more pain and, in the case of abuse, more and more dysfunction. Monica was *not* retraumatized by remembering even the most frightening details of her abuse. Her many tears did not plunge her into an abyss that she could not get out of; they brought relief and helped create the doorway through which her essential self (the part of her that was there before any abuse occurred) could emerge. In all the years I have been a therapist, I have never seen anyone retraumatized by remembering and reprocessing the painful experiences that have tormented them all their lives. It might hurt to set a broken bone, but when it is set, healing begins. What I most want you to remember from Monica's story is that for many of us, burying our pain, while it is our psyche's attempt to protect us, has the unfortunate side effect of burying that essential, innocent, alive part of us along with it. This is exactly why both victims and perpetrators are so often unhappy people, even if they put on a good front or have developed many compensating behaviors like workaholism, making lots of money, or having a huge crowd of friends. Opening to the true sources of pain and working them through helps us reconnect to our most alive, authentic selves, and if you have had that experience, you know there is no substitute for that.

Facing pain takes courage and strength, and in the process, we grow our courage and build our strength. This is one way we build character and develop the tools to cope constructively with whatever life brings us as we go on. As we face pain and learn how to work through it, we no longer need to project it, numb it out, or act it out. This is a core principle of psychological healing. **Feeling pain is, therefore, a means to an end, not an end in itself. It is the beginning of the healing jour-**

ney, not the end of it. In good psychotherapy, we're not building pain tolerance; we're uncovering pain to release it and find healing on the other side.

America looks up at me helplessly from beneath her crown. *I'm in pain,* she says. *What can I do?*

Feeling Our National Pain

It is no different for us as a nation than it is for an individual or family. We need to face our national pain as an essential part of healing as a country. If we were able to stop denying it, minimizing it, and blaming others—and I realize this is a far stretch in and of itself—where would we start? Well, together, we would start with our present symptoms like we would with any client. In America's case, she tells us she is suffering from escalating mass murders, as seen in the CNN article that mentions there were four hundred mass shootings in the US by July 2023, hostile and verbally violent division of political parties, hatred and violence among racial, religious, gender, and economic groups, high levels of pollution, corruption, and greed, and a severely imbalanced economy with a handful of wealthy people and millions of poor . . .[37]

We dive in, starting with where America began. We talk about how the original settlers came to America for many reasons—as we explored earlier in this book. They brought with them not only their strengths and skills, but *they also brought with them their traumas.* And out of those traumas, they severely traumatized others—Native Americans and Black people being some of those we horrifically abused. The legacy of all that unhealed trauma is alive and well today and repeats itself as a cycle of victim and victimizer, and the wheel of abuse keeps spinning.

Our ideals of political and religious freedom, our industriousness and spirit of adventure, our gifts, and even our love have been colored by the pain we fled and the pain we inflicted, exactly as it is for any given individual or family.

The Family of America is a melting pot of nationalities, with our diverse histories, conditioning, traditions, values, and traumas, whether we like it or not. This is what we bring to the table of our human relations, and just as we do in therapy for the individual and the family, we must look together as a nation at what happened that brought us to the suffering we are experiencing today. We face the pain while we remember the good. America once carried a torch that welcomed the tired, the poor, the huddled masses yearning to breathe free—the same people who came to America to begin with. And then something happened, and we forgot, and many of us do not want to remember, just like so many of us bury our pain and do not want to delve into the traumas of our individual pasts. We have not learned how to face all that pain without blame, resentment, and rage, and that is exactly why we are still experiencing it and acting it out on one another the way we do today.

I imagine America sitting here facing it all, remembering the wounds we have felt and the pain we have inflicted, *and,* like Monica, uncovering our greatness. We have the opportunity now to find the victim inside the abuser in us as a country and face and embrace both. We could face and embrace all that we fled and all that we brought, all the pain and all the wealth of spirit and tradition that got buried under our defenses, our projections and prejudices, our competitive impulses, and our addictions to wealth, power, and control. America, like each one of us, has her collective wounds to heal and so much of great value to share.

Facing and releasing pain and all the negative beliefs and projections we have absorbed over time—these are the keys to uncovering the greatness we contain. One of the most valuable gifts of the best therapy is that the therapist holds that there is an essential self in all of us waiting to emerge and flower, as Monica discovered. And that to get to that gold, we undo the destructive family dynamics that buried it. This is the very opposite of focusing on our injuries and failings with the intent to judge, condemn, and punish. We focus on what hasn't worked and isn't working to get to the essence that lies beneath and find what does work. The good news is we do not have to be therapists to do this for one another. We don't need a degree. We need to unearth the gold in ourselves and hold that light for one another. This is the safe passage that good therapy gives us to rediscover and reclaim both our inner and our outer homeland.

Perhaps it wouldn't be so hard to face all the abuses in our national family if we knew the goal was not to find the culprits and hate them but to look them in the eye, tell our truths to ourselves, be fully accountable for the impact we have had on each other, and together uncover the riches in all of us we have buried. So many of us brought massive trauma with us when we came here. Along with our hopes for a new life in a new land, we also brought pain, greed, and prejudice, and we had no idea we would end up acting all that painful conditioning out on ourselves and others. We didn't have a psychological understanding of ourselves in those days, just like I and all my clients didn't have that understanding when we were young. But we have it now, and it's not too late for any of us or our country to heal.

Our history and our conditioning have everything to do with our mental health and well-being (or lack thereof) in the present—our personal history and the history of our country. Ask the many Native Americans whose ancestors were slaughtered, their land taken, their children kidnapped, horribly abused, and often killed in the "schools" they were forced into. They will tell you that they are still trying to recover from the abuses of the past, as well as those that persist in the present. And we know how much past pain and trauma affect the present from the studies of post-traumatic stress disorder among returning soldiers who witnessed mass deaths and killed people themselves. They were traumatized by the wars waged by the human family, just like little Justin and Carol were traumatized by the wars waged in their families, only these larger wars left thousands of real people dead, injured, homeless, and orphaned. We know now from the severity of their symptoms—among which some of the most common are flashbacks to traumatic incidents, suicidal thoughts, panic, nightmares, numbness, and rage—that many service men and women have not been able to go on with life as usual. One study revealed that 83% of service men and women and active respondents have experienced PTSD since 9/11.[38]

And we are waking up to the fact that mass shooters are not happy people. The Violence Project, run by Dr. Jillian Peterson and Dr. James Densley, is a non-profit and non-partisan organization that is funded by the National Institute on Justice. It researches mass shootings and has developed an interdisciplinary approach to gun violence prevention, mental health crisis intervention, and training for law enforcement in the de-escalation of violence. Their research found that the vast majority of shooters had experienced childhood trauma and had witnåessed violence—a parent's suicide, sexual or physical abuse, domestic violence, neglect, and extreme bullying. It was also found that many were experiencing a present crisis, had seen mass murders in the media, and had examples to follow (Peterson and Densley stated that mass murder is now "socially contagious"). This quote from their study was particularly disturbing: "Once someone decides life is no longer worth living and that murdering others would be a proper revenge, only means and opportunity stand in the way of another mass shooting."[39] Once someone decides *life is no longer worth living*—this is what we want to pay attention to, as individuals and as a country. When a person feels life is no longer worth living, they are suffering severe pain and unhealed trauma at human hands. Their despair and their impulse toward violence is their Cry for Help.

We are back at the beginning of our discussion. Facing our own pain and learning how to make it safe for others to face theirs, with a focus on healing rather than blame and punishment, is the key to the cure for our country.

Chapter 8:

EMBRACING DEPENDENCY FOR HIGH-TECH HUMAN RELATIONS

What we need to understand is that abuse is both caused by and perpetuates broken bonds. When we harm others, we break the bonds of connection between us. In the very act of abusing another is the message that I don't care about you. I don't care about your pain, your loss, or even your life. This is the essence of a broken bond. Nothing *attaches* me to you. I am *detached* from you and from your welfare. This leaves the door wide open for more abuse, exploitation, destruction, and, ultimately, the use of weapons, both psychological and physical. When we talk about upgrading to the most High-Tech Human Relations, the urgency to do so is really the urgency to preserve human life and, with it, all life as we know it on earth.

We depend on each other to survive. The most fundamental bond we come into the world with is our dependency on our parents or family unit to keep us alive. Our physical and emotional welfare depends on that mutual attachment being safe and consistent. As we mature, we learn to navigate between appropriate dependency and growing independence. But somehow, the idea of dependency in human relationships has been undervalued, overlooked, and considered a sign of weakness. How many clients have I had whose partners won't come to therapy because "they don't *need* anyone's help," or who have hesitated to seek help themselves for years, even though their marriages are falling apart or their children are in trouble? How many times have I heard people tell me the thing they fear most is to appear "needy" in their relationships or that they are afraid of becoming *dependent on therapy*? We're not afraid of becoming dependent on a doctor, car mechanic, or cell phone company. We know we need them for resources, skills, and expertise we don't have ourselves. But when it comes to the helplessness we experience in meeting our vulnerable intimacy needs with other human beings—when it comes to mending hurting hearts and broken relationships or resolving conflict—suddenly, we are terrified of having to rely on anyone who might possibly see our "neediness," admitting there are times when we are at a total loss, or fear we have failed. When clients tell me they don't want to be needy, I say, "Why not? We're all needy." We all want and *need* something from others. The question is not whether I should need you or how much. The question is, is it safe to need other people? Can I embrace my needs and the needs of those around me constructively and as an *adult*? What might that look like, and how exactly do I do that?

Healthy Dependency: A Key Feature of High-Tech Human Relations

Healthy dependency is not the same as co-dependency, which can be described as extreme emotional dependence on a partner in which I need the other person to be okay so that I can feel okay. It is a dynamic in which I sacrifice myself to ensure your welfare because I don't believe I have what I need to make it on my own, emotionally or otherwise. Co-dependency is often the underlying dynamic keeping a person feeling dependent on an addict or an abuser. But it must be understood as a symptom of a wound to a healthy, safe connection that manifests as insecurity and a preoccupation with the supposed welfare of others that is, in fact, a desperate cry to be taken care of oneself. It is a symptom of unmet, legitimate dependency needs.

The opposite of co-dependency is fierce and resolute independence. *I don't need anyone.* But this, too, is a symptom of unmet legitimate need in relationship. It is a predictable response when our normal needs for love, belonging, safety, and being provided for are ignored, shamed, punished, or met with violence and abuse and, sometimes, all the above.

It is just a fact that we need each other more than we allow ourselves to know. For one thing, we simply cannot survive on our own. I don't grow all my own food, generate electricity, or pipe in water. I can't take out my own appendix. I cannot escape the undeniable, most basic truth that I need a whole world of others to keep the air I breathe breathable and the water I drink clean. I *depend* on and cannot live without many of the services, supplies, and protections our highly complex technological, industrial world affords me.

At the same time, we want to be sure we can take care of ourselves if we lose a relationship, a job, our health, or our savings. A certain level of independence and self-sufficiency is a marker for adulthood. But that said, let's look at our development here in America from a different angle. While we are infatuated with the ideal of greater and greater independence, we are *more dependent* for our survival on a far greater number of other people than ever before in history, people here at home and millions of others around the world. At the same time, our determination to keep the ideal of independence prevents us from acknowledging this fact. Somehow, we manage to avoid the terrifying implications of that dependency in the most convoluted and sophisticated ways. Our ever-growing ability (in our culture) to own our own cars, our own phones, our own

TVs in our own rooms, our own personal trainer, our own, our own, our own . . . perhaps has deluded us into thinking we are independent when the opposite is true. We couldn't have any of this if it weren't for all the thousands and millions of people who make this "independence" possible. Our conditioning is so focused on the idea of autonomy that it does not prepare us for the increasingly complex dependencies we must come to terms with as adults. It does not prepare us for what dependency looks like in an adult form here in the twenty-first century or even to acknowledge it as an issue.

Embracing Emotional Dependency: A Sign of Strength

All this autonomy does not factor in that we need each other emotionally as much as we need each other to meet our basic survival needs. We need love and belonging as much as we need a home and food on the table. We need safe, meaningful community with one another as much as we need clean air and water. We need help from other people when we are depressed, anxiety-ridden, raging, addicted, and lonely. Yet acknowledging the depth of our need for one another, for many of us, has become marginalized, minimized, shamed, and in many ways denied.

We need emotional connection with other people, but we are not "supposed to" need too much or let it show. We're supposed to be okay alone, focus on loving ourselves, and not expect to have our needs met by others. These are relevant concepts at certain times and in their place. But their place is within the context of relationship. **We are in relationship with one another whether we like it or not, whether we want to admit it or not, and the quality of our relationships directly affects our moods, our coping strategies, our ability to function, and our health.** We are in relationship with our partners and children, employers and co-workers, friends, law enforcement, congressmen and women, presidents, oil producers in the Middle East, and cell phone manufacturers in China. We need them all. And we need them to be safe for us, to factor us into their equation in some viable way. We need them to care. We depend on that bond of human connection. When the bond is broken, we may be in emotional, if not physical, danger. We need to be able to admit that the impact of broken bonds on us is tremendous, that it causes pain, and that our coping mechanisms are sometimes as harmful to ourselves and others as the hurt we have endured. We need to be able to say we need help from other human beings to find our way back into love, connection, and cooperation. Therapy teaches us how to say we need help. Most importantly, we desperately need societal as well as family permission to be vulnerable, to need others, and to embrace that understanding as a strength and not a deficit. We need to make it common knowledge that meeting each other's legitimate dependency needs for love and belonging, safety, and cooperation is critical to our survival.

It is a part of the climate of abuse and neglect in our country (and worldwide) that has so many of us worshipping independence or submissively serving others in hopes of getting our genuine needs met. In a healthy family, we are safe to rely on each other emotionally and physically, and we also learn to take care of ourselves—both. In a healthy family, there is a balance between caring for others and being cared for.

Interdependence: Autonomy Meets Dependency

What we know from the best psychology is that healthy adult dependency can best be understood as embracing our *inter*dependence. We need others, and they need us. But how we are to actualize our interdependency with the whole—the immediate community and the entire world—is not so well prescribed in this culture. The focus is still, to a large extent, on how I will make it, on me and mine. The dependency aspect of our development, both as individuals and as world citizens, has been systematically ignored, undervalued, and misrepresented with the sudden onset of a highly industrialized and technologically advanced social order that idealizes becoming financially independent and, therefore, without "need." We have made a giant and overnight leap away from a focus on cooperation as a means of mutual survival to glorifying independence. And, sadly, those who are left behind—those at the bottom of a skewed economy who do not earn a living wage and who cannot afford healthcare or higher education—are often judged as inappropriately "needy" by society, as needing from our social order what that they should be independent enough to provide for themselves. At the same time, ironically, the more we feel insecure in our ability to sustain ourselves in a society so self-focused, the more the need for independence feels like an utter necessity.

The time has come to face and embrace our true interdependency with one another. Surely, we're not dependent on *everyone*, you might say, not every single grocer or orphan halfway around the world. But I would have to argue that the September 11, 2001, terrorist attack on America showed us, if nothing else, that it just might be that very individual who is finally fed up at not being taken care of by the collective, at being hated for his race or religion, who could suddenly become ripe to be swooped up by the next group of equally fed up cast-aways from *our collective consideration*. This individual may even then move to America, enroll in flight school, and only want to learn how to take off. It took so very few discontented individuals to turn a world of billions upside-down with 9/11.[40] And out of that incident, which killed 2,996 people, including the nineteen terrorists, it is estimated that over 360,000 civilians were then killed in the subsequent "war on terror" launched by the Bush administration. We cannot afford to go on thinking that every single living being doesn't matter to us all. We must find a new center of gravity, a new place from which to stand if we're going to stand at all. We must become accountable for ourselves *before* the next bomb falls.

Acknowledging dependency is anything but a weakness. It takes courage, strength, and willingness to risk disappointment and hurt to *feel* our dependency, embrace it, and speak it. *I need you. We need each other.*

The fact that many of us find that level of dependency a liability has everything to do with why we, as a nation, are where we are—more and more isolated, defended, and at war with others and ourselves.

What we need to acknowledge for ourselves—that we need each other—is what we need to acknowledge as a country. America needs all other countries, races, and religious groups to make it safe for us to survive here—and they need us to make it safe for them. Nuclear weapons will not make us safe. We know this, and yet, we deny it. What will it take for us to truly get it that we may not survive without facing and embracing our interdependence with all human beings and reconfiguring our national and international human relations?

Abuse Makes Dependency Dangerous

In looking at the dynamics of abuse and how they have warped our beliefs and ways of coping, what becomes clear is that we find dependency threatening when our authentic needs for one another have been violated. Abuse makes dependency dangerous when those we depend on have the power to hurt us, withhold what we need, hate us, and assault us. Abuse makes dependency dangerous and counterintuitive when to have even basic needs met, we are forced to submit to violence and violation, please or try to avoid the abuser, or sacrifice our voice and our integrity to survive. This is the sad legacy of abuse, whether it is abuse in a family or abuse by a government. When our legitimate needs for acceptance and belonging, a living wage, adequate housing, medical care, physical safety, and social justice are withheld, scoffed at, violated, and silenced, we will not want to acknowledge our needs. They have become a liability. **But the answer is not to deny our dependency, either as individuals or as a country. The answer is to do everything in our power to meet the legitimate needs of all of us the best we can.** This is yet another crucial element of High-Tech Human Relations. It is the basis for cooperation with one another for our mutual good. The commitment itself, even if we don't know how to do it, and even if it will take time, would be a game changer. If the most oppressed among us (those who have *needed* us the most) knew their cry was heard and that there was a commitment to meet the needs that have been denied, we would already have a different America and the path to a different world.

Creating a New Political Language

In a way, you could say embracing our dependency on one another requires an enormous shift from a very masculine I-can-take-care-of-myself approach to human relations to incorporating more of what we consider feminine feelings of connectedness and vulnerability. While it is not within the scope of this book to delve into the issues of patriarchy and feminism per se, I believe you will see that these issues are, nevertheless, addressed at their core in the following chapters. It has been considered feminine (and, therefore, "weak") to talk about love and her attendants—safety and peace. It is not by accident that these words are not part of present-day political discourse. The language of politics in America is a language of domination and submission, competition and conquest, opposition, opponents, and war. Without reference to the language of peace, safety, and love, **the language of politics in America today is on a continuum to the language of abuse.**

Marianne Williamson, a widely published author, thought leader in spirituality, and political activist, decided to run for president in 2020. Previously, she founded Project Angel Food in 1989, a non-profit that has delivered millions of meals to sick and dying patients in their homes. The goal of the non-profit was to help people suffering from AIDS. Marianne Williamson has also worked throughout her career on poverty, anti-hunger, and racial reconciliation issues. In 2004, she co-founded The Peace Alliance, and she has supported the creation of a US Department of Peace. Her career is testimony to her commitment to listen and respond to the cries of the suffering and create peace in America.[41] At the 2020

Democratic presidential debate, she said, "Mr. President, if you're listening, I want you to hear me please: You have harnessed fear for political purposes, and only love can cast that out . . . I'm going to harness love for political purposes. I will meet you on that field, and sir, love will win."[42] She was openly calling out abuse tactics in politics and taking a stand to bring love onto the playing field of America at the highest level.

She received a lot of interest initially for her alternative take on politics but was also widely mocked. One Twitter user wrote that Williamson was proposing a healthcare program based in "witchcraft."[43] It is both fascinating and horrifying that the use of the word love, coming from a woman who called out a man, brought up the specter of *witchcraft*—that the values of love and care associated with the feminine were immediately dismissed as suspect and dangerous. Much of the mockery painted Williamson as a sage-burning flake or someone who would sprinkle crystals on the debate stage. All because she spoke of love! Williamson braved a politics of abuse to talk of love as a national agenda—exactly what has been missing that has put us all at such great risk! "A politics of love," she said, "is not a path of passivity or weakness. It is a path of radical truth-telling, refusal to look away from unnecessary suffering, and a courageous rejection of criminal, economic, and social injustice. Only big truth will have the power to defeat big lies."[44] She was talking about High-Tech Human Relations, but the roar of the crowd drowned her message.

Williamson didn't make it very far on the debate stage, but what we need to know is that she tried to bring fierce, bold love into the pollical conversation, and she was met with a lot of disdain. If love and the safety and peace that follow in love's footsteps are going to have their rightful and most urgently needed place on the political table, we must free them from outdated associations of "feminine weakness," hippie superficiality, and witchcraft. We can and must do better.

Fully facing our interdependency with one another is the door we need to pass through to create a sustainable world for ourselves and all future generations. Why? Because it is the withholding of what we depend on each other for most that is our deepest wound—as individuals and families and as a national family. The things we depend on each other for are actually all the elements of High-Tech Human Relations. We depend on each other to meet our *needs* for love and belonging, basic necessities, connection, cooperation and sharing, safety, and peaceful ways to resolve our differences. These are the bonds that hold us and keep us together when we are challenged, stressed, angry, and afraid. It is the withholding of our legitimate dependency needs that is at the heart of our pain and dysfunction—as individuals and as a country.

Let me say it to you this way, I tell America. *In my marriage and with my children, family, friends, and clients, I would never think to say, "Make Me Great Again!" I think about who I am for others in relationship and who they are for me. I'm certainly not holding myself up as a paragon of virtue, but what I have learned from all the trial and error of my life is that feeding the bonds between us is what makes us great, not focusing solely on ourselves. Embracing dependency is the life raft we need to get to shore.*

This is my prayer, too, America says. *That we really come to understand how much we need and depend on each other and that it becomes our strength. My prayer is that we find our greatness in who we are for everyone here at home and around the world.*

I can see she wants to light her torch. She is looking for a match.

Chapter 9:

REPAIR IS THE HOPE FOR OUR COUNTRY

O*kay,* America says. *I hear the Cry for Help; I feel our pain; I see the need to embrace and honor our dependency. I'm ready for what we can do next.*

Human relations can be so easily disrupted. Most of us know from our own experience how quickly our feelings can be hurt, how right we can believe we are, and how angry and insistent we can become. It was the fall of 2006; the man I was about to marry and I had one of our worst fights cleaning out his pantry. I wanted to throw away, and he wanted to save. I don't remember now what we decided about all those glass jars that, in my view, had been sitting empty or half-filled with fossilized pinto beans for the last twenty-five years. I hope I was the one to give in, but I probably wasn't. I hope we made a compromise, but I can't remember now.

God knows what we ended up screaming at each other, but at just the right moment, he threw a big plastic bucket onto the tile floor, and we both started laughing. The crazy irony of it was that we were getting the house ready for our wedding! Thirty years earlier, in my first marriage, I probably would have left the house and not come back until it was too dark and lonely to keep walking away. But I was sixty-two at this point, thousands of dollars and countless hours of therapy (and a graduate degree in Psychology for me) later, and we still had the fight! We still got caught up in the very important struggle for control of which old glass jars got thrown out and which ones didn't. But absurd as this may sound, I think all that therapy and all that scratching our way up and out of our most hurting places paid off in that moment of laughter. I think it took all that personal work not to turn our catfight into a small Greek tragedy. In its own microcosmic way, it was a moment of genuine salvation that came before anyone was crucified. The salvation was that we dropped the argument and reconnected with each other and our love. That is the whole point of Repair. It is the pathway to reconnection with one another, and reconnection is the strongest foundation for healing our broken bonds and restoring us to peace and safety.

In my relationship with my now-husband, we usually find that beneath the overt issue, the way we are communicating about it, which is usually some form of a power struggle, has opened a wound in one or both of us—a place we felt unheard, abandoned, or put down—wounds we have with domination and submission we carry with us into adulthood. In short, beneath the overt issue, we usually find a wound in our connection to others. One small step at a time, we learn to communicate better, end the tug of war, and grow our empathy for ourselves and each other. We have learned through trial and error that finding our way back to connection is what matters most. **Repair means we use everything we know to reconnect as quickly as we can without abandoning ourselves. It means the relationship itself is the sacred container within which we do our work.** And when we are at our very best, which is not always, we understand that the ways we trigger each other can be reframed as opportunities to strengthen our own self-control, stretch the limits of tolerance of our own and the other's distress, and deepen our empathy for our very human fallible condition. This is the salvation we so desperately need in America and worldwide—that we hold the relationships we have within our country and with the world as the sacred container in which we have been given the opportunity to evolve our consciousness into High-Tech Human Relations and ultimate sustainability for humanity. In the process, we learn to repair the breakdowns we have created and create the conditions to minimize or prevent them as much as humanly possible in the future. We learn to step back, take control of ourselves, and keep communicating before anyone gets crucified. What my husband and I keep learning is that the satisfaction of being right is dimmed by the sweet taste of all the love available in moments of actual cease-fire and reconnection. This is my hope for America and humanity.

Human beings will continue to disagree, have conflicts, and get angry. It is highly unlikely that this will change. In the best of circumstances, we work things out, but often, we give in, and sometimes, we overpower each other to get our way. Sometimes, we stay at war for long periods of time, with no one winning anything. Men and women, races, economic groups, and countries have been fighting for years with no resolution. Throughout this book, we have looked at the tremendous and life-threatening toll these wars take on us as individuals and groups. We've looked at the toll on our children, and we've brought to light how the unresolved traumas of battle get handed down from one generation to another if not interrupted. We've looked at how power struggles, even if won temporarily, do not bring lasting peace or renew connectedness. They may bring a cessation of battle, but only until the next one arises.

The diagnosis is in. It is time to pull out all the stops, come together, and use everything we know to heal our collective mental and emotional state that has put us at such great risk. In words we can all understand: **Repair means we find our way back to connection with one another**.

It is the loss of loving connection that is the source of our deepest wounds and dysfunction. Repair, then, is not possible while the dynamics of abuse—Low-Tech Human Relations—are alive and well. Blame, threats, refusal to listen, retaliation, and violence are the dynamics of abuse that need to be repaired! We start by calling them out. We have done that. Now it is time to talk about what I and so many others have learned from the field of psychology that can help bring us back to safety, peace, and love. This is Repair.

What It Means to Repair

Repair means we fix something that has been broken or damaged, and we put it back together so that it works again. This is clear-cut when we are talking about a car. We add in the fluid that is low, or we buy a new engine, or we replace the brake pads. Repairing human relations— restoring us to High-Tech Human Relations—to safety, peace, and love, is much more complex. It is not an exact science. And like all aspects of human relations, Repair happens on a continuum. On one end of the spectrum, it might look like we barely reached a truce, but we are not fighting anymore. Somewhere in the middle, we have talked and listened, we understand each other better, and we have agreements, but we are still invested emotionally in our side of the conflict. Toward the end of the continuum, we have a deeper understanding of one another, the con- flict has dissolved, *and* we feel reconnected; we feel our caring for one another. All possibilities are good. All serve safety, peace, and love. A truce is a big step away from war. Listening and understanding take us another step toward reconnection on an emotional level, which is the goal of Repair in human relations. Reconnection brings mutual care. It is one of the most gratifying, joyous feelings a human being can experience. I care about you, I feel cared for by you, and you feel the same with me. Our desire to hurt one another or be at war disappears and is replaced by the desire to reconnect as soon as possible when we fall back into conflict.

The old paradigm of blame and retaliation is transformed into the *desire* to come back together. This is High-Tech Human Relations.

If we can train people to build rockets and transplant organs, surely, we can teach each other how to communicate respectfully and come back together. We don't have to do it perfectly, and we won't. We just need to keep trying. Terry Real, a well-known couples therapist, says relationships are a process of rupture and repair. As individuals and as a nation, we know how to create rupture—we're experts at it! In fact, most of us have been taught that coming out on top, winning an argument, or being able to get our way are signs of strength or worth. It is only now, as we find ourselves facing a fragile and uncertain future that we are being asked to evolve out of a win-lose, right-wrong consciousness. The point is that we will have ruptures. We will not see eye to eye on all things. We will be working out the often-conflicting needs not only of differing individuals but of the individual in relation to the whole and of countries in relation to one another. But we don't have to be taken out by our disagreements. And the more we understand that our very lives and the lives of our children depend on working together to resolve our differences, the more we will be committed to returning to Repair, to healing, no matter what it takes.

The Role of the Therapist

A therapist stands outside the stuck dynamics inside you and in your relationships with other people. As therapists, our goal is to create an emotionally safe place for you to speak your pain, your needs, and your most uncomfortable truths, whether to yourself or to another person. Our goal is not to judge but to help you go deeper to uncover the sources of pain and find repair. We do our imperfect best to make it safe to face your anger, fears, and most dysfunctional behaviors while guiding you toward healing your wounds and creating more life-giving and relationally healthy ways of being. We help cultivate empathy and compassion for the pain of self and others to reach common ground. For many of our worst conflicts and pain, we need an outside, neutral third party to guide us. Facilitation can be life-changing; therapists help couples stop fighting, rekindle love and affection, and learn the skills to come back to safety when they lose it or separate more peacefully. We help families navigate the complexity of child and adult needs, and we help individuals work through depression and anxiety and learn to manage fear and anger. Not perfectly, but much better than before outside help was sought.

Trained facilitation provides someone outside the system who holds the conflicting parties to the ground rules, ensuring restraint of our aggressive impulses while teaching new methods of nonviolent communication and conflict resolution. There are many models for this work, but the common denominator of them all is that we learn to listen to others the way we want to be heard. There isn't one among us who doesn't want to be heard and validated for our feelings and points of view. Our biggest problem is that we don't know how to listen. It is almost counter-intuitive, it seems, to back off and give the other space to be heard because we become so insistent on being heard ourselves. Deep listening is one of the skills most urgently needed in families, workplaces, and in government. Otherwise, we have an endless battle of wills. Nonviolent communication skills, then, are one huge element therapists use to make it safe to disagree. We succeed some of the time, and some of the time we don't, but with the model of peaceful conflict resolution we can learn in therapy, we have a place to return to and try again.

There is a lot more to say about the role of the therapist that I will share with you as I go deeper into Repair, but to start, I want to say that many of us do not know how to navigate the intensity of interpersonal conflict and unprocessed trauma and, especially, the pain of abuse alone. In fact, most of us don't. It is, therefore, critical to have help in the form of someone who can guide us and point the way. It is critical to remember that the worst injuries we are trying to recover from are those we have suffered at human hands, and they need to be healed with human hands held out to us. This is the job of a therapist, but as you will see as I continue, it is a job we can learn to do for one another. We are here together to take therapy out of an office and into the world!

There is nothing esoteric about anything I am about to share with you about Repair, but while the principles of Repair may be easy to formulate, they are not easy to embody in action, especially when we try to apply the principles of Repair to a nation. It is, in fact, easier to make war. Resolving conflict while maintaining and re-establishing relatedness is far more difficult.

Six Elements of Repair

There are six basic elements of Repair to focus on when we have conflict: restraint, responsibility, reflection, rehabilitation, resolution, and reconnection. They are all part of the best psychotherapy, and while they overlap, I will outline each one separately for you. To be clear, these principles apply to conflict that does not involve overt danger to any party. You will see these six principles repeated and expanded as we continue, but let's start with an overview. Many of the elements of repair have been written about and are already being implemented in our therapy offices and now in some of our schools, places of business, divorce and custody mediation, and in conflicts on local and broader levels by people aware of the urgency to come together to work out our disagreements. The bigger challenge comes in making these practices widely understood and practiced, especially on a national and international level. I will outline some of the basics to begin with and, from there, move to the implications of practicing Repair as a nation.

Restraint: Restraint is the first element of Repair. One of the first things we learn in therapy is that we must leave our weapons at the door. Restraint means we restrain ourselves from violence—from verbal, emotional, and physical assault on one another and from self-harming behaviors. When a couple comes to therapy, we let them know we will stop them if they become verbally violent or threaten harm. When people are feeling reactive and upset, and they don't feel in control of what they might hurl at each other, we teach them how to call a timeout for themselves to calm down. We ask them to make a commitment to return to the conversation when they are ready to listen the way they want to be heard and speak the way they want to be spoken to. This can be very difficult when we are fired up and when I'm sure you're wrong and I'm right. It sometimes takes a huge act of restraint and self-control to abide by this guideline, but without it—even if we must stop and start again, which, being human, we often do—we are just repeating the aggression and pain that hurt us in the first place and that we have likely been acting out at home. Most of us did not learn restraint or nonviolent conflict resolution skills growing up. We learned to fight, submit, distance, retaliate, avoid, and go around each other. Many of us never had the experience of sitting down in our families and talking directly about problems and solutions, but today, with our deeper understanding of family dynamics and the powerful influence of caregivers over the lives of their children and with the attention being paid to the terrible effects of bullying and gun violence, mediation programs have sprung up to help us navigate conflictual divorces, employee/employer relationships, and the scapegoating and bullying among young people.

With that being said, I doubt there is any one of us who has not, at one time or another, been so angry or hurt that we could not stop ourselves from screaming, slamming a door, or storming out. Maybe throwing something or threatening divorce—or worse. If you have, you know how extremely difficult it can be to control your behavior and come back to the table. Sometimes, it takes hours or days. Sometimes, we limp back, hoping to be received, or, in the best cases, we finally see where we can take responsibility, and we summon up the strength to admit our own part and ask forgiveness. For all those who claim that peace is for the weak and the passive, I say that the strength it takes to exercise restraint of our most hurtful and violent impulses is far greater than any supposed power inherent in verbal and other forms of assault.

Good therapy provides and teaches us how to create for ourselves a safe container for communication in which one person speaks uninterrupted while the other reflects what they heard—without interpretation or defense. Then, the parties switch sides, and the listener becomes the speaker. Only then do both parties look together at the requests that have been made of them about what they each need for healing. Only then, in the space of deep listening, does the conversation about where they can agree or give what is being asked for take place. And it takes restraint to do this. Ask any couple who has done this kind of work how hard it is not to interrupt—how much self-control it takes to listen without defending or even walking out!

My husband threw a plastic bucket at the floor, not at me (we have never thrown anything before or since). We didn't say cruel things to one another or make threats. We basically just lost our cool, and I'm grateful that all that aggression got channeled safely in a way that we could both laugh. Was that the best model of restraint? Hardly. The challenge to navigate our power and control issues is ongoing. But I tell you this story because I want to be clear we are imperfect human beings, and perfection is not the goal. The goal is Repair! Whatever we do to restrain and redirect our anger is a win if it brings us back together.

Responsibility: In any given conflict, most of us can see quite clearly what the other has done wrong, and usually, we are bound and determined not only to point it out to them but also demand they see whatever happened the way we do and admit it. The difficulty is that the other person feels the same way—they want us to see and admit our fault in the conflict, and we end up in a tug of war. One of the hardest things to do is listen, take in the other person's point of view, and find one thing we can validate for them. Unless one of us is being totally unreasonable or abusive, both parties have something valid that needs to be heard. With my husband, this is still sometimes very hard for me to do. It is the nature of intimate relationship that we will trigger each other's deepest wounds and, therefore, our deepest unconscious reactions, coping strategies, and defenses. That is what happened with my husband and me in the glass jar incident. We weren't really arguing about the jars, even though it looked that way. We had both been terribly overpowered as children, and that silly disagreement brought all the genuine injury to our personal power to the surface. What most of us who have been hurt by another did not get was the experience of the raging, critical, unavailable, or abusive parent (or other) taking any responsibility for what they did. We long for that now, and we demand it from our partners and others. But we are adults now, so Repair means we learn to give the other what we (and likely they) did not get. The bridge back to one another, forged by taking responsibility for our own part (their valid complaint), is what heals us both. Even if it's after the fact! Even if the argument wasn't really about what it appeared to be, and even if we yelled and the plastic bucket got thrown. It's never too late to take responsibility for ourselves.

When I was in graduate school in a class on couples counseling, our instructor said that in all his years as a therapist, the couples who fared the best were those in which each partner focused on their own contribution to any given upset and on what they could do differently. This doesn't mean I can't say that I was upset that you didn't call when you knew you would be late or that you can't tell me you are angry because I spoke in a harsh tone of voice. But we talk about our upsets with each other in terms of their impact on us, not in terms of judgment of the other. Then, we both take stock of the other's complaints, and we work on what we ourselves can do differently. Repair depends on self-responsibility, which often takes the form of making "I" statements instead of "you" statements (which can come across as blaming). I think, I feel, what I would like is . . . and what I am willing to take responsibility for and do differently is . . .

The focus is on taking responsibility for our part in the conflict, on being courageous enough to own our missteps, feel the impact we have had on others, and begin to formulate and commit to what we will do differently. In the case of an abused spouse or child or a tortured population, the focus is not on them assuming responsibility for what happened but on being supported to tell the full truth of what they suffered, share the depths of pain and violation within the safety net of a facilitated container, be heard, and be responded to. But for most of what I am addressing here about responsibility, I want to emphasize that one person can lead the way. If I can own my part without blaming you, you will likely feel safe enough to do the same.

I am talking about broad outlines here. The conflicts we need to face and resolve here in America range from localized issues to urgent international concerns—anywhere from disputes over the minimum wage and healthcare to environmental safety, racial discrimination, defense, and our role in international relations. The conflicts still raging have as much to do with our past as with our present—slavery, gender inequality, the role of police and the military, how we have used and treated nature in the larger picture of diminishing resources and climate change, and on and on and on. It is not within the scope or purpose of this book to go into them all or to pretend that any model of communication has all the answers we need. The scope and purpose of this book are to look fearlessly at the psychological dynamics of abuse that have created life-threatening problems in America, discuss the ultimate gains of healing our hearts and minds, and highlight that the path to resolving even our most entrenched issues begins with the desire for Repair and the tools to implement it.

We can't change the past. I can't change the fact that I yelled at you when I should have been listening more empathically. But I can learn from what I did. I can listen to the pain you felt and the impact I have had on your life, and I can learn new ways to behave when I am upset and commit to them. We cannot change the fact that our ancestors here in America killed hundreds of thousands of Native Americans, stole their children and their lands, and enslaved as many African Americans and hated, tortured, and defiled them as human beings. We cannot change the fact that we have objectified women, blamed them for rape, and legislated inequality. We cannot change any of what we have done in the past, but we can face it now. We can listen to the impact of what we have done without blaming our victims and without shaming them for their symptoms of depression, hopelessness, anger, and failure to thrive. We can hear the Cry for Help now and feel the empathy that we did not feel in the past. And most importantly, we can stop the abuse—the hatred, blame, deprivation, and violence. We can stop the murder. We can stop the war. We have the choice to do now for others what we did not do in the past. The more we commit to being accountable and to taking responsibility for what is ours, individually and as a nation, we can do the work of Repair.

Reflection. Responsibility and reflection go hand in hand. I must be able to look at myself and not be totally focused on you and whatever I believe you did to have even a prayer of seeing my own contribution to our conflict. I must be willing to see things about myself that are uncomfortable or don't fit the image I have of myself or want others to have of me—my own critical nature, impatience, anger, or intolerance. But this is exactly what we want from others! We want them to see and acknowledge their shortcomings and all the ways they have hurt us. Repair means we learn to give to others what we want them to give us. Repair means we learn how to reflect on ourselves and take responsibility for what we see that might not be all that wonderful.

I can say this with some humor, but, in fact, self-reflection can be very confronting and sometimes excruciating. It can inspire self-blame and shame—"I'm such an idiot! Why did I care about the pinto beans? I'm ruining my wedding! Why would he want to marry me?" Or we resist seeing ourselves at all and keep blaming the other person. "He's a hoarder and a control freak!" The more we can restrain ourselves from shame and blame of self and other, the more likely we both will be able to reflect honestly and fearlessly on ourselves. In our pantry argument, my husband and I could both reflect in an instant, laugh, and come back together. When the trigger is deeper, or one of us is still "in it," or the perceived wound is greater, the strength it takes to look at myself can feel like climbing Mount Everest. And it's okay. We're human, and we keep trying. The fighting is easy; the Repair is hard work.

To reiterate, reflection is part of taking responsibility. To take full responsibility, I need to be willing to reflect on what motivates me and how I come across in the words I choose, my tone of voice, my body posture, the look on my face, and the actions I take. These are all forms of communication. Words alone are only one part of my communication that I learn to reflect on and be responsible for. If I were to say, "I hear you," but my voice is flat, my body posture is stiff, and I am not making eye contact with you, it is highly unlikely you will feel heard or validated by me, and it is even less likely our issues will be resolved or that we will feel any sense of Repair. Self-reflection does not occur in our thinking alone, and it is not as simple as a word change, though that may be where it needs to start. In the pantry fight with my now-husband, I had to acknowledge that my problem was that I wanted things done my way, that I didn't want my opinion to be challenged, and that I can be very judgmental about the way other people do things. I also had to acknowledge that I become insistent and pushy and that I wasn't interested in any other point of view than my own. And I had to be willing to reflect on the impact my pushiness was having on the man I was about to marry. These are issues I still work with to this day. Reflection is a lifelong process.

Self-reflection may be one of the greatest challenges we humans have ever faced. It is certainly one of the greatest challenges we face here in America—finding the courage to keep our focus on our motives and behaviors and what our impact has been on others rather than blaming them. If you have ever had the experience of moving into fearless honesty with yourself, you know that it will prompt you to change your whole approach to the other person (the last thing we want to do when we are caught in judging and defending). We will be prompted from within to move our body toward them rather than away, relax the tension in our face, soften our voice, and look undefended into their eyes. Sometimes, it takes everything we've got to do this. Yet it is just this open emotional quality—when we can access it—that is most likely to result in our "opponent" softening their stance as well. I've witnessed this countless times, both as a therapist and in my personal life. I hope you have been blessed to have the experience of someone doing this for you. But if you haven't (and many of us have never had it, witnessed it, or knew it was possible), I hope you will come to know, through embodying it yourself, how powerful this level of self-reflection and responsibility is for healing our relational wounds.

Therapy for America means we take it upon ourselves to be the ones to do the hard work of self-reflection first in our own lives and in our national politics. I've outlined many of the most pressing issues we have yet to reflect on and take responsibility for as a nation, as well as the abuse dynamics on the individual and national levels that still stand in the way of our embracing this critical phase of the Repair process. Our work is to create a mental and emotional climate in our homes and in our country where it is esteemed, safe, and rewarded to be self-reflective in all the ways described above.

Rehabilitation: The act of rehabilitation, or making amends, can take many forms. It could mean a sincere apology, an act of kindness for someone we have hurt, paying back money, or returning something that was stolen or damaged. It can take the form of a commitment to behave differently in the future, like committing not to walk out or slam the door when upset, put down our phone and listen when the other is talking, or do more around the house. Or it can be a commitment to get a job or go to therapy. There are two elements to rehabilitation that are important.

One is the action itself—returning the money or calling for a therapy appointment. The second is the emotional communication of remorse and a desire for emotional Repair. I let you know I am truly sorry. I feel the pain I inflicted, I am willing to reflect on my behavior, and I want to take responsibility for it and do what it takes to have resolution with you so that we can reconnect. This can happen in an instant of genuine apology, or it may take time to navigate the steps. If I only pay you back but don't communicate sorrow for my actions or be willing to hear my impact on you, it's perhaps better than nothing. But it doesn't get us fully to Repair. If I only laugh with my husband about the pantry incident but don't apologize for raising my voice, I haven't truly made amends. The goal of Repair is reconnection—a felt sense of our relatedness—because that is both what heals and what creates the foundation for greater relatedness and peaceful conflict resolution in the future. Making amends without reconnection is partial resolution, and it may be as good as it gets in any given moment, but we need to know that reconnection is what truly heals relationship, and without it, the foundation for safety, peace, and love remains shaky.

The very best amends we can make to anyone is to treat them differently now. What we most need in America is a forum in which to speak, listen, and be heard about the pain of centuries of violation and atrocity committed against so many populations and to do our utmost to hear from those who have assaulted and murdered others—hear their stories and what drove them to violence, and look for healing for them as well. This is a critical part of High-Tech Human Relations. The goal is to create a frame of healing for everyone. The goal is to shift away from the politics of blame and punishment to a politics of seeing the victim inside the perpetrator and seeking healing for that part of all of us.

The best example of how this might be undertaken in America on a national level can be found in the model of the Truth and Reconciliation Commission that was established in South Africa in 1995 to heal the country from three hundred years of colonialism and apartheid. According to an article in Britannica, the goal of the commission was to end apartheid and create a democratic government with elections and a constitution, and in the process, deal with accountability and reparations. The commission drew on wide public participation and provided the opening for both victims and perpetrators to come to the table, tell their stories, and speak their truths. It outlined amnesty, rehabilitation, reparations, and the establishment of a bill of rights. The primary focus was on victims, and the commission was open and transparent so that the public was made aware of the full extent of the atrocities committed during apartheid.[45]

I think it is noteworthy that it was called the Truth and Reconciliation Commission. There was a great focus on exposing the full extent of the truth of the atrocities committed under apartheid. The truth was owned. The commission was set up for deep and painful public reflection. Its creation was an act of taking responsibility and opening the door for amends and reparation. And, of course, it had flaws. Many in the highest positions of authority did not participate, and the economic abuse of apartheid was not addressed. Even so, it was the first commission of its kind to hear both victims' stories and perpetrators' confessions, not for the purpose of blame and retaliation but for the purpose of moving toward peace and reconciliation for all South Africans. It could be expected that it was not perfect, but it was a start in the direction of everything I am saying about shifting our focus and mindset from abuse to healing, from blame to deep listening, and from continued war to building the foundation for peace.

Can we ask ourselves if we would now be willing to have truth and reconciliation commissions of our own here in America—for Black people, Native Americans, women, marginalized communities, and all people who have been assaulted and misused by our abusive institutions, policies, and officials? This is the courage it will take to wage peace.

Amnesty was a condition for coming to the table by those who had participated in the abuses of apartheid. We may still want to have consequences for or impose restraint on the most dangerous perpetrators among us. But even that can be imposed with an attitude and a goal of rehabilitation, of helping restore to psychological health the person inside the murderer or the thief. Why? Number one is because committing to the rehabilitation of offenders whenever possible is an acknowledgment that there are often larger social issues that set many people up to become the aggressor and the abuser (as discussed earlier) that have resulted in discrimination and poverty, and role-model violence. A commitment to rehabilitation is a powerful message that we are willing to take responsibility for societal abuse and neglect by offering help to many of those who have already been mistreated. The second equally important reason to provide rehabilitation is so that those released back into society have the best chance of recovering from their own wounds and becoming accountable in the present. Rehabilitation gives them the best chance of becoming safe and contributing members of the communities we all live in and safe and healthy partners and parents so that their wounds and dysfunction do not get passed on. Rehabilitation is one of the most effective ways we can interrupt the cycle of abuse. It is our best effort at prevention, and prevention is a key to cure.

But let's be sure not to draw a sharp line between "us" and "them." We all can be rehabilitated—from our poor conditioning, from our prejudices and judgments of others, and from our preoccupation with ourselves and our beliefs, needs, and biases. We can all be rehabilitated from ignorance of our own psychological makeup (and that of others) and our blindness to what harms and heals in human relations. This is the best prevention of abuse, and every one of us can be a part of it by being willing to look at our own role in perpetuating a psychology of blame, shame, and judgment and educating ourselves to take a more psychologically sound, compassionate, and healing attitude toward our fellow man. I cannot imagine there is one among us who does not right now have someone we could make amends to. And what joy it would be if we could celebrate making amends instead of feeling shame or defensiveness around what we have done. What if making amends—as individuals and as a nation—could become a goal, an investment, and a source of healthy national pride? I'm voting for that America.

Resolution: All the previous elements of Repair are what make resolution possible. In some instances, resolution may require no more than a deeper understanding of one another, and the conflict subsides all by itself, but more often, it requires an agreement, a path forward, something we commit to do differently, and learning new ways to behave. For a couple, resolution might entail a commitment to practice peaceful conflict resolution skills outside the therapy office, share parenting more equally, or make deep and lasting amends for an affair. For our nation, it is complex. We have so many ongoing disagreements, so many of our own people being wounded, and so many of us still doing the wounding. The dynamics of abuse keep too many of us from seeing the need for Repair. We are not close to resolution. We have all the foregoing steps to pass through. The hope is that we can talk about it and educate ourselves about how to identify and reverse the dynamics and the effects of abuse. Creating a Department of Peace and a Department of Psychology in America could be a step in the direction of making our psychological well-being a priority in our national agenda, departments of government that are schooled in High-Tech Human Relations that we infuse not only into the workings of government itself but into local politics, school curriculums, and job training, for example. We could easily create the courses Identifying Abuse 101, Basics of Nonviolent Conflict Resolution, and Peace, Safety, and Love Studies, not as forced subjects but as an investment in our own welfare and sustainability. The creation of such departments would be an acknowledgment at the national level that we need help from the top down and the bottom up to come to the table with the commitment to stay at the table until resolution is reached. Such departments could be the hub of our own version of truth and reconciliation, formulating plans of action to resolve both long-standing conflicts and reparation to all those who have been the victims of national abuse. Our hope lies in whatever form of truth and resolution we can come up with.

Reconnection: Reconnection is the last big element of Repair. The first steps of Repair make it safe, desirable, and possible to reconnect to one another. Reconnection is the goal and the prize of the hard work of Repair. When we feel connected and have a sense of belonging, we desire to cooperate and support the welfare of everyone—because we belong to everyone. I believe we all want the experience of belonging. And when there isn't something life-giving and kind to belong to, many of us will join whoever comes along and takes us in, even if they are dangerous, hateful, and destructive. The Hope for Our Country is that we see this now, that we understand and can have compassion for ourselves and all others. What we really want to belong to is love.

Reconnection heals all wounds. There is nothing like the feeling of coming back together after anger, hurt, and disagreement have torn us apart, nothing like the feeling of safety, peacefulness, and love when anger has subsided, and we can feel our belonging to one another again. I hope, dear reader, you have experienced this often in your life, but if you haven't, you deserve to. We all need and deserve to live with other people and in a country that is committed to reconnection within our human family. It is the healthiest food for human beings. We are not made to be islands, and the adaptations we make when unresolved anger and abuse tear us apart create some of our most dysfunctional symptoms, as I have described in detail earlier in the book. We are wired for love and connection, and I will talk more about that later. But for now, I will say that there may be no greater pain than when the bonds of human connection are broken. Abuse breaks those bonds, and High-Tech Human Relations restore them.

You can see, can you not, that we have all the tools we need to resolve our deepest divisions, hatreds, and the suffering we have both created and endured. We are not deficient in the how-to. What we need more than ever is the commitment to Repair, but even before the commitment comes the desire. We must want it, and right now, we must want it bad. What brings most people to therapy is pain—pain that is so bad it has become unbearable, so bad we are willing to get help and try something new. The list of terrors we face as a nation, including terrorism itself, should be sounding an alarm that is impossible to ignore, but the dynamics of abuse have prevented us from hearing the Cry for Help from our fellow humans and from the earth. We are still being taught to threaten, silence, and even kill our truth-tellers, we are afraid to stand up to the abusers, or we get high off their power and brainwashed to join their ranks and are rewarded for complying with them. These are all the dynamics of abusive families playing out in national politics that keep too many of us from facing the threats to our own survival.

There is only one response to abuse that works, and that is to stop it. This book is a call to arms in that sense. But I don't want to imply battle or suggest a war against anything or anyone. I am proposing that we wake up and see what we are doing to one another and what is being done to us. We cannot repair the climate of abuse in America if we cannot call it out for the terrible impact it is having on us and the danger it puts us in. The more people who can call out the abuses of our nation with a desire for Repair, the greater the call and the more possibility it will be heard. This is the Hope for Our Country and, really, the hope for our world.

This book is my best effort to find a balance between exposing the severity of abuse dynamics in America and igniting the deepest, most heart-felt joint effort possible to find the cures and commit to them. The bridge from terror to hope is one we need to cross to one another.

What I am proposing as Repair for our country will be the hardest thing we will ever do. It will be the most challenging yet the wisest and most life-giving endeavor we have ever undertaken. It will require more from us than exploring new worlds, creating new technologies, or peering into the farthest reaches of outer space. It will be an exploration, a re-examination, and a reworking of our last frontier—inner space—exactly what the best therapy helps us do.

All the elements of Repair are what will bring us true liberation, which is freedom from the oppression of abusive family systems. We have tasted this liberation as individuals through psychotherapy and other healing modalities, and many of us are already taking it to our families, friends, and the communities we interact with. Our work now is to take it to our country.

This is why I hold a torch, America tells me. *I am lighting a way. You might have thought my torch was a beacon for the weary seeking our shores, and it was, and I hope it will be again. But my torch is now the light we need on the path through the darkness we have created ourselves—the abuses here at home so many of us are fleeing with nowhere to go unless we point the way.*

Good, I say. *Let's continue our work then by looking at the Case for Safety, Peace, and Love.*

Chapter 10:

THE CASE FOR SAFETY

I will start where all good therapy starts—and hold on—because it will be confronting. I talked about how the therapist makes it safe to tell our stories, reveal our pain, and face the uncomfortable truths about ourselves that we have hidden or denied. The therapist helps us feel safe to be vulnerable, frightened, angry, and sad. A safe container in therapy normalizes our feelings of dependency, confusion, and blockage and helps us move behind the façade of having it all together that we often feel we need to face the world, do our jobs, parent, and be there for others. Safety is multi-faceted, and, in fact, whether we are in therapy or talking with a friend or going to the dentist, we have our radar out all the time (usually unconsciously) measuring the level of safety we feel with others—to be ourselves, express our needs, voice concerns, or disagree. Our radar becomes activated as the level of unsafety increases, and we either move into defense mode or we do our best to use the skills we have developed to navigate feelings of threat with whatever we believe is constructive and minimizes conflict. That skill set is made up of the elements of Repair. Allowing ourselves to work through our ruptures in a safe place and then focusing on Repair is what brings resolution and reconnection with one another.

When we take these principles of High-Tech Human Relations to America, the first things that come to mind are ground rules for creating the safety necessary for negotiating with those we are in conflict with. Without that bottom line of what constitutes safety and a commitment to return to it when we lose it, it is difficult, if not impossible, to resolve anything. Everything we know about healing our families and individual relationships depends on nonviolence. This is ground zero for healthy relating. We leave our emotional weapons at the door. This is not all there is to safety, but there is no safety without it.

What this means for America is that if we want to get on the road to healing the abusive mindset and behaviors that have put our own citizens, other nations and races, and our planet at such great risk, we need to create the same guidelines for ourselves as a country, a government, and as leaders. No therapist sits by idly and lets clients insult each other or raise a fist. We don't let people come into the office with a gun. To repeat, abuse on any level is what is causing their problems, and it will never be part of the cure. **America in Therapy means disarmament.** If you were thinking that applying the rules of the best therapy and healing work to America would be easy, that we could perhaps institute a policy of mediation sessions—and that certainly would be a huge step forward—I cannot in good conscience say that would be enough. It would be tremendous, but it would not be enough.

I know there are many people who think the idea of disarmament is preposterous, who take great pride in our military prowess, or who will say disarmament is fanciful thinking and that it will never happen. But this is exactly what we are all up against—the mindset that believes safety depends on killing untold numbers of people every day. I'd person-ally rather not have to say something so controversial. I know it will take a 180-degree shift for many of us to understand that it is the *psychologi-cal* state of mind that believes in the use of force, justifies abuse, blames its victims, and believes in war and killing that poses the greatest threat to our ultimate survival. We will only be able to make this shift when enough of us realize that the case for creating true safety in our country has been misrepresented as a partisan political issue requiring the unlim-ited use of force when, in fact, we are dealing with a mental health crisis that requires a whole new perspective and set of repair skills. We will be on the road to true safety when we realize that *psychological health—* High-Tech Human Relations—are what will bring us both personal safety and, ultimately, national and global security.

I want you to remember, dear reader, a time when someone you were at odds with was able to drop their defenses and hear you. Or maybe it was you who calmed yourself down and was finally able to listen and take in another's reality. Wasn't it the most wonderful feeling in the world to feel safe to be open, authentic, and heard or hear another and reconnect? There is something so deeply rewarding and healing when we are fully heard without the "But you . . ." coming back at us. And that kind of lis-tening is what opens the space to give it to the other.

My client Jen had been in a very conflictual marriage. When she and her husband fought, they usually yelled at each other for a short time and then iced each other out with angry silence that could last days. Then, they would haltingly come back together without talking about what hap-pened. Eventually, they got divorced. Jen got a job at a mental health agency and became good friends with a co-worker, Larry. One day, Larry sat her down and said he wanted to talk about something that was bother-ing him. Jen's defenses rose to the surface. "Oh no," she thought, "Here it comes." But Larry put her at ease right away. He told her calmly what he was upset about with her and what he would like her to do differently in the future, and then he invited her to talk about her perception of what had happened, what she felt, and what she needed from him. When the conversation ended, their friendship was renewed. That conversation, she told me, changed her life. She had never had the experience of another person making such a conscious effort to handle conflict safely, respectfully, and with an obvious desire to work it out with her. In that moment, she literally set herself on a path of reworking how she dealt with conflict and upset for the rest of her life.

Not many people learned these skills growing up. For the most part, we learn them in therapy or mediation or, if we're lucky, in good relationships. Not often do we witness the basic skills for psychological health being modeled in public or political conversation. Imagine if we had these rules of engagement in local, state, and federal government and if candidates running for office and elected officials were not allowed to insult each other or post threatening images of their opponents—in short, if they were not allowed to behave in ways that would have us fired from our jobs or would have our children be suspended from school. Imagine if they were taught and required and helped to sit down with their opponents and listen the way they want to be heard!

The book *History, Art and Archives, United States House of Representatives* includes the story of "The Most Infamous Floor Brawl in the History of the US House of Representatives." It occurred on February 6, 1858, during a debate about slavery. Two representatives of opposing parties insulted each other and then exchanged blows, and over thirty other House members joined the fray. Nothing was settled, and the brawl itself was a sad predictor of what was to come.[46]

Three years later, the Civil War began, in which it is estimated that 750,000 men died, 476,000 were wounded, 400,000 were captured and missing, and 50,000 civilians died. Though the records are known to be incomplete, we do know that more men died in that war than in all the other wars America has been engaged in combined.[47] This is the real human toll of our inability to commit to safety in debate with guidelines we follow to work out our differences.

Our present-day legislature is mirroring some of our history of resorting to attack on one another. Elected officials tear each other down verbally on almost a daily basis. Americans are all too familiar with these antics being reported in the press or on social media. Verbal violence of this kind is both a product of an abuse mentality and further fuels it, making it impossible to sit down and safely work out our differences or find resolution. This trend in America today is a cause for great concern. As our "leaders" display this behavior, their constituents mirror it. Social media is awash with name-calling, a divisive us versus them mentality that encourages teens to post gun-toting videos and adults to broadcast threats of violence and civil war. These are alarm bells we desperately need to hear, and they are also a Cry for Help. They let us know how urgent it is that we do the work to make it safe to disagree.

If we step outside the overt divisions in policy and practice between Red and Blue and look at the *dynamics* playing out on the political stage through the lens of psychology, the first thing we need, if we really don't want countless deaths of innocent people and another war, is a commitment to nonviolence, disarmament on every level. The fact that we are not horrified and not loudly calling for High-Tech Human Relations and a commitment to peaceful conflict resolution in our government's behavior, no matter what it takes, is a sign of just how pervasive the effects of mass individual and institutional abuse are in America today, just how mentally off balance we have become. We must allow ourselves to know the toll of human life we are implying when we even mention civil war.

Many years ago, I was fortunate enough to attend a talk by an international mediator named Craig Barnes. He said something I will never forget. He told us that when he sat down with conflicting parties, the first thing he asked them to do was to tell each other what pain they had endured at the other's hands, the injuries and starvation they had suffered, the loved ones who had been killed, and the homes and sacred sites that had been destroyed. He created a safe space for them to express the pain that was fueling hatred and violence, and this opened the door to empathy. This, he said, was the critical first step to mediation being successful. It required a "cease-fire" on both sides to be possible. This is what I am talking about. And it is not pie in the sky: it is possible if we put our guns down, both literally and figuratively.

Imagine if, in Congress and in local and state government, there were mediators present at every session to moderate discussion of opposing views and hold a space of non-judgment that fostered deep listening and directed all parties toward resolution—for the sake of creating safety in the midst of disagreement for the Family of America!

When I talk about disarmament being the number one condition for creating safety, I am not only talking about leaving our emotional weapons, verbal violence, and threats at the door of any conflict or negotiation. I am talking about actual disarmament. Period. This may be one of the most confronting issues for America today. **Disarmament means disarming nuclear and other weapons of mass destruction and not building more of them.** It means redefining the role of the military and retraining police to use force only when all other options have failed to provide protection. It means teaching nonviolence to our children and funding nonviolent conflict resolution education for adults, businesses, and other social institutions. It means a national commitment to do everything in our power to negotiate conflict peacefully, which is the only real safety. I know there are a million "what ifs" that come to mind when I propose this. I know this is not something that can happen overnight. I'm saying we need to make disarmament the goal, the destination, and we figure out the route all along the way by starting in our homes and communities and doing everything we can to repair our human relations.

Think of it this way. Imagine trying to discuss an upset or disagreement with your partner or boss while there is a gun poking through their pocket or they are openly holding a gun to your head. How safe would you feel? How open, honest, and hopeful of being heard and met would you feel? America is holding guns to the heads of our neighbors, using weapons against some of them, and holding guns to the heads of many of our own citizens as policy, as practice, and as threat. We cannot go on this way and hope for any different results than the ones we are already getting—poverty, racial hatred and persecution, mass murders, terrorism, and war.

The Dance of Power

There is a lot to take in here. When I talk about the Case for Safety for all Americans, especially literal disarmament, I am talking about a subject that many people would argue is either foolish or beyond the realm of possibility. I would argue this way. When a boat is sinking, some people will grab seats on the lifeboat without a thought for those left behind. Some people will give up their seats and be willing to face a watery death to save another's life, which is, of course, laudable. At the same time, some will try to find a way to save everyone, whether we know exactly how to do it or not. The rise in violent polarization, continued investment in war and weapons of mass destruction, and environmental policy and practices that create life-threatening changes in our climate might tell us this boat is sinking! And part of what is pushing us under are all those who say there are no leaks in the boat and refuse to stop the leaks we see. For the rest of us, there is no seat we can give up to save another life, no lifeboat beyond imagining we can stay safe a little longer where we are and pray someone else will figure out how to save us later. What is left is to try to figure out how to *save us all.* That is why we are having this conversation. There is one boat that could float us—healing our psychological state—so we want to build it big and strong, with room for everyone.

Maybe it's too late, America says.

But what if it's not? I reply.

In that vein, I want to share with you something I learned in my role as a therapist that no one taught me in graduate school. I learned something about the issue of power that is critical to our survival. We live in a win-lose world, a domination and submission model of human relations that relies heavily on forcing others into compliance with our ways of thinking, with our beliefs, and with giving us what we want. This world is all about having power over others, a *power-over* dynamic, as I call it. The therapy model teaches us something quite different about power that I want to share with you because it may mean the difference between life and death.

The power differential between people is part of our daily experience. We cede power, take power, and do our tugs-of-war, or we cooperate and share power, mostly without thinking about it unless it becomes a problem. And we do this Dance of Power as part of our survival. One up, one down, and hopefully some of the time on a level playing field. We tend to do the Dance of Power with others the way we learned as children from our caregivers and from the power models of our present culture. What we most suffer from in America today in this regard is the increasingly lethal model of power-over, of taking power from others and keeping it. This model of power is part of the operating system that allows massive abuse, as discussed earlier. I want your money, so I charge you a huge fee for something you need. I want your body, so I enslave you or seduce you or rape you. I want your allegiance, so I brainwash you, hold you hostage, or pay you off. Or it may be much more subtle. I want to feel superior, so I slip little boasts about myself into my conversation with you. Or I want you to need me, so I hint at your weaknesses and the ways you are less proficient at something than I am, or I put down your other friends so you will rely on me more. It can feel good to have power over others. It can be its own kind of "high." It easily becomes an addiction, and, like all addictions, it is part of psychological ill health. The primary relationship of the addict, in this case, is with power itself, *not with people*, which is a setup for abuse of that power. We need look no further than what the United States has done historically to Native Americans and Black people, exercising power-over in ways that destroyed peoples' lives, tore their families apart, and, in the case of Native Americans, took their land and resources. We have a long history as a country of taking from other people the power to determine their own governments, economies, and social orders. Again, it is not in the scope of this book to explore the full extent of how America has usurped power from other nations and people. But it may be illuminating to know that while we threw off the yoke of colonization from Great Britain ourselves and have taken great pride in our fight for independence, we ourselves are colonizers. When the word colonization came to be taboo, we called the lands we took possession of "territories." Hawaii was taken as a "territory" in 1898 and didn't become a state until 1959. As of this writing, US territories include Puerto Rico, Guam, American Samoa, US Virgin Islands, the Marianas, and Wake Island. The Philippines was a US territory until 1946. And Puerto Rican citizens, now considered American citizens, are subject to US law but cannot vote for the US President, have no congressional representation, and yet, they are required to serve in the military.[48]

But we don't have to look outside our borders to see how we continue the power-over dynamic today with women, the poor, and non-white people. In an article by Curtis Bunn for NBC News, it was stated that in 2021, 27% of those killed by police were Black people, who make up only 13% of America's total population.[49] Other research by Brookings found that Black people are fatally shot by police at three times their relative share of the population and twice as likely to be killed by police as white people.[50] As of this writing, our government has yet to pass the Equal Rights Amendment, which would guarantee equal pay for equal work for women. This is a way of holding economic power over women. And injustices past and present toward Native people in the United States have led to poverty, addiction, substandard education, and substandard healthcare. These are just a very few examples illustrating that the power-over dynamic creates a system in which safety is clearly not guaranteed for all.

In our psychotherapy offices, we practice a very different under-standing of power that is in sync with High-Tech Human Relations. The therapeutic relationship implies a certain power differential, like any pro-fessional relationship we have with someone who has a skill we can't provide for ourselves. In a sense, you could say that, as clients, we hand over some of our power to the therapist. We depend on them to help us. If therapy is to work, we drop our defenses and let them in. They get an intimate look at our pain, our insecurities, and our traumas. We give them the "power" to help us deal with the complexities of our entire internal psychological makeup, our history, and our unfulfilled dreams. This makes us very vulnerable to the therapist's influence. The safeguard against any misuse of the power we give the therapist is this: **a good therapist doesn't take the power we give them. They "hold" it while we release, reprocess, and restore—to ourselves—what was injured or taken from us.** They help us work through the ways our legitimate dependency needs were not met or violated at an earlier time. A good therapist knows we will not need them forever to heal but that, like a doctor, they may help clean out a wound and help us bandage it up. In the process, they help us find our own resources and healing power within ourselves. They don't give us the message we need them forever. The therapist may hold the back of the bike until we find our own balance, but the goal is for us to find our own balance, our own ability to handle our lives. The bike belongs to us. We're supposed to ride away.

Many years after my divorce from my first husband, I saw a lovely therapist named George for yet another round of therapy. I had a powerful insight while working with him. I told him I had always believed I would be alone forever, but I finally realized for the first time that this belief was not a fact. I didn't get born under a curse that said I would be alone forever. There was no prediction from the Oracle of Delphi. While there were real events in my childhood that generated this belief, its pervasive power lay in the fact that I had never questioned it. Something in the therapy with George snapped me out of that trance, and in that breakthrough moment, I was a little bit like a prisoner unexpectedly let out of jail. I remember the light in his office that afternoon and his gentle face that seemed to sincerely wish for me that I could find love, and I took that feeling home with me. There was such release from years of self-isolation that my depression lifted. After a few more sessions, I felt I no longer needed to see him weekly, and I told him I would like to start coming every other week. Shockingly, he said no, that he only saw people weekly, and suggested I continue with weekly sessions. I was confused and taken aback. Therapy had helped me find a lost piece of myself. I felt new possibility! I thought George might celebrate with me, but it was his way or no way. So, I left because it felt like he was holding onto the back of my bike, and I wanted to test my own balance. For some clients, weekly sessions are necessary for long stretches. But for me, at that time with George, I knew it was time to rely on my own resources. In the best therapy, this change in the process would involve a conversation of deep listening between client and therapist that would be a part of the therapy itself so that the power differential would not be ignored or misused in any way.

George was a wonderful therapist, and no real harm was done. He wasn't perfect. I'm not either, but I understood even more deeply the subtle play of power that can occur, even in a wonderful, non-toxic relationship. He held the power I gave him very skillfully for the most part, but there was just a little piece he didn't know how to return, so I had to take it myself.

Safety in the therapeutic relationship means we can depend on therapists not to repeat our original wounds, which generally were caused by some misuse of power over us. The goal of therapy is that we leave much more able to access our strengths and gifts. A good therapist is happy when we are ready to end, even though it means we won't be paying them anymore. When a client thanks us for our work with them, we say, "*You* did amazing work. And thank you; we were a good team." We take joy in seeing them reclaim their power and become the agents of their own ongoing recovery process. And we are not the judge of when that moment comes; our clients are. From the first moment of the first session, we are helping the people we work with *outgrow* therapy. We know that the power they give us to help them belongs to them. Our clients are not safe with us if there is any other agenda.

My work with James was all about the interconnection of safety and power. Years of brutal abuse by several men in his family left him timid and passive to the point of virtual paralysis in even mildly stressful situations. He could barely speak when we first met, and he often stopped mid-sentence, unable to complete his thought. James shared almost nothing of his present life with me except to say he came to therapy because he was having nightmares with imagery he could not explain. James never missed a session, yet he barely spoke. It was as if he just needed another body there with him as the echo chamber in which his own voice came back to him. I knew instinctively to wait, breathe with him, tolerate the long agonizing silences, interpret nothing, and ask only the most gentle, open-ended questions. Two years passed as tiny fragments of abuse emerged, like sharp teeth slowly tearing an opening in his cloak of protection. We were in the Dance of Power. It had several parts. The obvious one was if I would be a safe container for all James needed to remember. He had to know I could handle the tremendous power he was giving me— that I wouldn't freak out, that I would believe him, and I wouldn't blame him. I knew the underlying question was not ultimately about me. I was the stand-in, you might say, for what he needed to know for himself. *Am I, James, a safe container for my own terrifying truths? Can I tolerate my own pain and believe my own memories? In the meantime, I need to know that you, Phyllis, have the power to hold everything for me until I find the power to do it myself.*

As a therapist, my job is often to hold what feels intolerable until the person I am working with absorbs enough caring from me and uncovers their own buried strengths to hold it themself.

Interestingly, but perhaps not surprisingly, James imagined me as a tiger. He didn't tell me this until we were well into our therapy. He needed me to be death-defyingly powerful if the torture he endured was ever going to reach consciousness. When he revealed this to me, James was still grappling with the shame he felt about his need for the tiger imagery, and I assured him again and again the day would come when he wouldn't need it anymore. By sharing this with me, James was asking me to enter a very vulnerable part of his inner world, which meant trust that I would not misuse the power he lent me was building. It was a great step in his therapy. He knew I wasn't a tiger, of course. He knew in a fully functioning corner of his adult mind that I was an ordinary human being but that he had to see me as all-powerful and all-knowing to tolerate his terrifying memories. Had I not understood what he was doing, I might have imagined I owned the power he gave me, that I was a superstar therapist who was going to be his savior, so great was his need and adoration of me. But we know better in the field of psychology, and we do our very imperfect best to hold power, not take it. Together, James and I could eventually acknowledge the utter necessity of his projection while we both also acknowledged it for what it was—a projection, like an image formed from light in a darkened room, shining behind an open hand, making its silhouette appear huge against the wall on which the most profound shadow play would be enacted. James and I held this image together for a long time until the play was finished, the lights went on, and the hand could be seen as just the size of his own.

James' trauma was the result of the torturous ways he was *overpowered* by abusive people. His power to protect himself, get away, and get help were all taken from him. An essential part of what heals abuse, in addition to reprocessing the trauma itself, is that all that power is restored to the one who has been injured. An essential part of healing abuse is having a new experience of power that is safe with another human being.

Many clients have a sense of self that is intact enough that they neither idealize the therapist nor give them undue power, or if they do for a short period of time, the therapy itself restores them to their selfhood without the issue ever being named or discussed. So why is this issue important? Because those of us who have had our power forcibly wrested from us, subtly or overtly (especially early in life), will too often give our power away without knowing it, or even if we recognize this dynamic, we're afraid to take our power back. We know how to be one down. We have been taught not to trust our instincts. We already feel less-than. We believe we need someone else's approval to feel good about ourselves. We are afraid of angering others. We have no experience of conflict ending well. This is the setup for abusive people to continue to overpower those who have already been traumatically overpowered. A good therapist knows this and knows that the restoration of power to the person who has been violated is critical to their healing.

In yet other instances, we come to get help, but we won't give the therapist any power at all. Kate was a highly intelligent, successful woman who, no matter what I said, even if I repeated back exactly what she told me word for word, would invariably give me a quizzical look and say, "No, that's not what I mean." Kate had no idea her door was shut tight. Feeling so unsafe in relationship and so afraid of being overpowered from living with both a raging father and an angry husband, she couldn't let anyone in. That was our work—how to make it safe for her to give up a little power and control and feel reassured that it would not be taken from her or misused.

One day, I very gently told Kate I was pretty sure I had repeated what she said. I asked her if it sounded different when I said it. Had I missed something? Was the tone of my voice off? Did she have a reaction to hearing her own words spoken by another person? Kate protested at first.

"Can you tell me again what you said?" I asked her. "I really want to understand."

Kate started to repeat it and stopped. She burst into tears.

"No one ever understood me," she said. "I tried to tell them, and no one listened."

Kate had finally opened her door, and we were able to dive into the pain of early abuse that was behind the wall she had built so high.

Whether we give our power away too much or don't give any at all, we will unconsciously dance with our therapists some form of the Dance of Power we have been taught and danced all our lives. **But what we really need to know is that we are already dancing that same dance, reenacting that old story, with everyone we are already in relationship with. And they are dancing their dance with us!** We are already, as individuals, groups, and nations, dancing some form of the Dance of Power—who takes the lead, and who is trained or forced to follow? We have yet to learn how to hold power for others when it is necessary, with the conscious intention always of returning it to its rightful owners—each other. Our world situation is now calling us to hold power delicately, like a bird with a hatchling in its mouth, carrying it to a more hospitable environment in which to grow into its own fully empowered adulthood.

I imagine you know where I am going with this, dear reader. I am saying that we haven't learned how to hold power *for* and *with* one another. We take it, or it is taken from us. Reworking our relationship to power is a crucial step in our next evolutionary challenge—to evolve our consciousness. Why? Because, as I have said many times throughout this book, the ways we exert power are now disastrous in our homes, deadly in our streets, causing unending violence and suffering in our nation, and life-threatening to the planet. I want to burn this last statement into our collective consciousness: **Our belief in and addiction to power over others is killing us.**

Evolving to Power-With

The epidemic of power-over, like any life-threatening condition, is calling us to find a solution or a cure. Historically, both power-over (conquest) and cooperation have been required for survival. But over time, we have perfected our ability to conquer to the point where we have become mass murderers. There is no known check and balance to what the explosion of one nuclear bomb can cause in an instant—the hundreds of thousands of lives that can be obliterated and the poisoning of whole swaths of our environment. This makes us all unsafe. We will not be safe until we understand the urgent need to radically transform our relationship to power. The only solution is to evolve our operating system from one of power-over to one of power-with. As long as we take power from others and don't return it, as long as we forget that it doesn't belong to us, that every human being has a right to use their own life force energy in the way they are called (unless they are a danger to themselves or others), none of us are safe.

I was able to learn this lesson clearly by being a therapist more than in any other relationship because the role of therapist is overtly not about my needs, wants, or desires. It is sometimes harder for me to remember to keep a balance of power with others in my personal life because my needs are very much at play in those relationships. But that is the work. This is how the principles and tools of therapy leave the office and enter the world we live in—with us. We don't have to become therapists to examine how we overpower others or let them overpower us or take power from them or give our power away. We can all begin to understand that the future of humanity rests on all of us reworking our relationship to power, starting with ourselves and everyone we interact with, starting with how we treat those we live with, who we vote for, and what policies we support in our communities and our country.

The idea that power-with rather than power-over is now critical to the safety and sustainability of all life is an evolutionary realization coming straight out of our understanding of psychology, if not from nature, science, and many forms of spirituality as well. It is a realization and a challenge that many people are not prepared to accept. Our resistance to relinquishing the power we have taken from others is perhaps unprecedented among all the challenges humans have had to face to survive. To rework our relationship to power will necessarily upend many of our beliefs, institutions, and the laws under which we now operate.

Let's imagine an America in which we hold power for and with others rather than take it. An America in which our members of Congress, for example, hold the power given them by the electorate as a sacred trust, knowing that the power belongs to the people, and they have been entrusted to use it in the best interests of all the electorate in mind. By this, I mean the interests spelled out by **High-Tech Human Relations**, our needs for acceptance, for our voices to be heard, for physical safety, for cooperation, to be provided for with food, housing, education, and medical care, for empathy, and for a legal system that is committed to justice for everyone and rehabilitation whenever possible. We would be asking nothing more of our government than we ask of parents—that they take good care of their children so that, eventually, their children leave home able to take care of themselves, are respectful of others (having internalized healthy boundaries), and are able to express their gifts and talents in the world. And the interesting thing is that when power is held appropriately and returned, and when it is then shared with respect for the other and within a context of safe and peaceful conflict resolution, it is far less likely to be abused. My experience as a therapist has shown me that healing the injury to our sense of personal power makes us safer human beings.

Oppressors, those who exert power over individuals and families or nationally and internationally, are unconcerned with the well-being of others, and they often believe they know what is best for everyone, but that is a fantasy (or an excuse) built on top of an addiction to power that is self-serving. What we have seen again and again as psychotherapists and others in the healing professions is that as people become safe and are given the opportunity to heal, *they* know what is best for themselves, and invariably, they become safe for others.

My client Tillie is a great example of bringing safety to the world around her through her own personal work. Tillie grew up an only child with a very unavailable mother. She always felt left out of whatever the in-group was. Divorced, lonely, and struggling herself as a single mother, Tillie got a job as a manager in a small office. A woman came to work for her who was noticeably insecure, anxious, and very much a people pleaser. Tillie couldn't stand her. She got great pleasure from ignoring this woman, overlooked her for work opportunities, and withheld any praise, even if it was deserved. Finally, the woman quit, and Tillie was more than happy to see her go. Tillie remembered all this as she was processing the pain of how ignored and left out she felt as a child. She remembered being on the playground in fifth grade, mortified that she was the last one picked for a baseball team. Then, the memory of how she had treated the woman from her office came bubbling up, and she sobbed with the realization that she had gotten pleasure from deliberately inflicting the pain of rejection on an insecure person like herself. Suddenly, she felt enormous empathy for this woman, whose very presence she had once found unbearable. It was in the safety and non-judgmental environment of therapy, where she could dive into her own pain, that Tillie could feel remorse for her cruel behavior and compassion for the woman she had hurt. In her role as manager, Tillie realized how much power she had to make people's lives miserable or gratifying just by the way she treated them. The unhealed wounds of her childhood made her unsafe as a person with power over others. We must realize that the unhealed wounds of many of those in power can make it frighteningly unsafe for those they control.

In therapy, Tillie was not judged for how she had behaved. Rather, the "victimizer" in her was offered a safe place to uncover the very hurting child in her, and in so doing, she could feel sorrow for the pain she had caused. She became warmer, more personable, and much more affirming of her employees as a result. She took the safety she had been given in therapy—non-judgment and deep empathic listening—with her out into the world, where she put her "weapons" down and created a safe space for others. This is how we take the healing possible through therapy into the world and become the agents ourselves of creating the world we want to live in, from the bottom up, from within the microcosm of our individual lives and the small circles of people we interact with. This is what we can and must ask of officials in our country, those who have been given the sacred trust to hold and use power for the sake of the people. Abraham Lincoln described democracy in America as a government "of the people, by the people, and for the people." This statement is a succinct way of talking about power shared for the common welfare as a structure of government and at the highest levels of authority. We have a way to go!

There are graduate programs in psychology and counseling that require students to be in therapy themselves. It only makes sense that therapists should experience the complex psychological dynamics, implicit vulnerability, and healing effects of the relationship they are to provide for others. Therapists have wounds, too, that can be acted out unconsciously on clients. Many responsible therapists do years of clinical supervision, in part to catch the ways they might be triggered by certain clients and, thus, more apt to "transfer" their own unresolved issues onto the people they are working with. Imagine that in America, we required government officials, who have power over millions of Americans, to work on their own conditioning in therapy, address their wounds, and access their greatest strengths. Imagine if therapy were regarded not only as a requirement for the job of leader but also as a privilege—to be given a place to not only examine personal power issues but also work through triggers instead of acting them out on countless others. Most jobs have requirements for education, training, or internships. A doctor won't be hired without years of schooling and supervised practice so that the doctor is safe to treat our bodies. I'd like to imagine how much safer and well cared for we would all be in America if we required our leaders to have training, not only in statesmanship and national and international affairs but in High-Tech Human Relations and peaceful conflict resolution. I'd like to imagine that our leaders would be required to do their own personal work and that, as a nation, we shared a deep understanding of both the harm we can do in an unhealed state and the good we can provide for others if we all had a safe place to address our unconscious conditioning and our wounds. And if we had the courage and wisdom to require that of ourselves!

When we are given the chance to peel back the layers of the power dynamics that wounded, repressed, and/or inappropriately over-empowered us, we become more caring, cooperative people like Tillie. We do not become hateful or greedy or need to dominate and hurt others. We simply do not. In all the years I have been a therapist, I have never seen it happen.

Help me understand, though, America says. *What can we do about all the violent abuses of power we cannot contain in the rest of the world, all the countries increasing their nuclear arsenals, attacking other nations, and putting tyrants in power as we speak?*

Many people have the same question, but what we need to understand is that America is one of those countries! We need to take responsibility for ourselves if we want to have any hope of influencing others in a new direction and making the world a safer place for everyone. We must start with ourselves. That is the point. If we want to end violence and tyranny, we have plenty of work to do right here in America.

The good news is that we have learned in our therapy offices that one person can change the dynamic for many. I have often had clients who want help with their conflictual relationships, but their partner refuses to come with them for help. What we don't often realize is that one person can change the dynamic of a relationship. If we don't grab the bait and fight back—if we take space until we or the other person calms down, make the first move to invite them to talk about what is hurting them, don't get defensive, attack, or blame, or set a boundary and tell them we are leaving if they cannot control their rage—*anything* other than engage in the old power struggle—there is a chance they will change their step in the old dance, too. It happens all the time.

I had a friend who was in a new relationship with a man who would explode periodically. She told him the relationship was a no-go if he didn't get help and control his anger. He went to therapy and did the work, and they have been happily married now for twenty years. Another friend was married to a man who was an alcoholic. They had four small children, and it was very scary but also courageous when she told him he could have alcohol or their family, but he could not have both. He hasn't had a drink in forty-six years. It can take just one person setting healthy limits and sticking to them while staying relational and connected to transform a relationship. Is there a guarantee? No. Some people will not make the needed changes, and by refusing to dance the old Dance of Power, we may lose a relationship we really wanted. But there is no lasting Repair on the individual level without safety. **The challenge on a national and international level and the big confrontation for America is that, unlike an individual who can get a divorce or move away, America cannot leave the earth if others refuse to cooperate**. We cannot threaten a divorce from planet earth or leave if others aren't willing to work it out. We share this planetary home with every other country, whether we like it or not. What is left for us is to change our step anyway, for Americans to become leaders of **High-Tech Human Relations** and refuse to engage in violence. We can be the ones to change our step in the dance of nations.

In an article in The Washington Post entitled *How the World is Proving Martin Luther King Right about Nonviolence*, peace activist Jamila Raquib is quoted as saying, "The greatest hope for humanity is not in condemning violence but making violence obsolete."[51] **We make violence obsolete by repairing and healing our human relations.** The article goes on to say that in an exploration of the efficacy of nonviolent protests and demonstrations, it was found unexpectedly "that campaigns of nonviolent resistance had succeeded more than twice as often as their violent counterparts when seeking to remove incumbent national leaders or gain territorial independence." Most of us don't know this. We have been taught that war is the way. Now is the time to unlearn what we have been told and get on the road to Repair.

The hope of this book is that by taking a deep dive into the nature of abuse dynamics and illuminating all we know about how to heal ourselves as individuals, we can be the ones to start us all on the road to safety.

America looks at me thoughtfully but with a softer gaze than before. I know the enormity of what I'm saying is starting to sink in.

I'm the one who has stood at our gates, she says, *welcoming hundreds of thousands who have fled war and the hideous ways human beings wield power over one another. I witnessed so much suffering and so much hope at the same time, especially when people saw my torch. But with all you are saying, I'm ready for a new job. I'm ready for the terrible reasons people come here to end and for us to make a new beginning.*

The Case for Safety in America does not, of course, cover all there is to say on the subject. It is just the beginning of a huge conversation. The next section continues where safety leaves off.

Chapter 11:

THE CASE FOR PEACE

You know, America says, *talk of peace has been characterized here as weakness, as something spaced-out hippies marched for back in the day and abandoned once they decided to get real jobs. Talk of peace is taken as a lack of respect for our veterans and all those who gave their lives fighting for our country. If we talk of peace, are we saying that their sacrifices were for nothing or that they were on the wrong side of history?*

I understand the question, of course. I do not question the sacrifice of the thousands of men and women who have fought and died for our country and for beliefs and ideals they held dear and believed justified the wars they fought. I am not diminishing their service or their suffering. Not at all. It is precisely because of their suffering, the suffering of their families and friends, and the suffering of all those killed on both sides of every war that I am making the Case for Peace. I am saying that it is peace that will put an end to all those unnecessary deaths.

The Case for Peace is not a case for passivity, powerlessness, or cow-ardice. Not at all. This is a big lie that must be exposed and undone if we are to survive here. Peace takes infinite courage and incredible strength to create and maintain, but it is not the strength of muscles and weapons. It is strength of character. It is the strength it takes to work through the prin-ciples of Repair with the goal of reconnecting to one another. It requires enormous self-control and determination to hold back when we want to lash out—when we want to hit someone or slash their tires or slam the door in their face. When we are committed to peace, we don't do those things—not because we are weak, but because we know the release of all that rage, fear, or disappointment won't get us what we want. It won't get us safety, connection, or feeling valued and cared for. It does not serve us any longer to see going to war as a badge of honor, a source of national pride. War is a symptom of Low-Tech Human Relations.

Peace is the hardest work of all. It is easier to fight and scream than it is to restrain ourselves and listen to what our perceived opponent has to say. It is easier and more automatic to fight than to take a powerful stand if need be in a way that does not close the door to others. Peace requires self-control in the face of hatred, bullying, and denial of our truths and our legitimate needs. If you have ever had the experience of holding back anger, barely holding onto the thin thread of commitment to a relationship when all you wanted to do was yell or storm out, you know how hard it is. You know how many times you have failed, but you also know how much more easily you can come back into connection when you take a deep breath and persevere or take a timeout before you try again. It takes *enormous strength* to exercise self-control and keep communicating until you reach Repair.

Pam was an intelligent and accomplished woman in her fifties who had no peace in her marriage. She sat stiffly in her chair as she told me how she kept shutting her husband out when they argued, and she couldn't seem to come back. She was triggered by not feeling heard and especially sensitive to feeling abandoned. Her defense was to stop talking and refuse to make eye contact. Pam froze as a child when her mother raged at her and then left her totally alone. In therapy, she was able to see that freezing in the present was an old response, but also, there was an element of revenge in icing her husband out that she admitted only after several sessions. She told me her husband would try to get her to talk until, finally, he would walk away in exasperation. Then she would feel utterly devastated by his abandonment! And eventually, they fought about that. In therapy, she saw that she was creating exactly the outcome she feared most—anger and abandonment. In a moment of clarity and courage, she asked her husband if, when he saw her shut down, he would just hold her. She told him she might not be able to talk yet but that she wanted to, and if he would hold her, she might be able to come back sooner. She said it took everything she had to ask for this, but in so doing, she felt like she had moved a mountain of pain and resistance. He agreed to try. Over time, Pam was able to unfreeze by herself and come back into the conversation. She marveled at what an amazing difference it was making in her marriage, how close she and her husband were able to become even after an upsetting disagreement, and how much peace she felt knowing and trusting now that they had a way back to each other.

It was easy and automatic for Pam to shut down, wall her husband out, and continue their war, but the consequences were devastating because the anger and abandonment of her childhood were being replayed in the present. It took inordinate strength and courage for her to move back into connection, but it healed the hurting little girl inside her, and it healed her marriage.

This is what I'm looking for, I tell America. *For all our warring factions to do their own work and find their way back to one another.*

As a country of warring parties, races, economic classes, and genders, and as a nation in conflict with other nations, we too often refuse to look at the cost of shutting each other out, walking away, and acting out our anger, judgment, and fear impulsively. It's almost like we doggedly focus on who won the last battle or how to win the next one, and we have blinders on to the massive trail of death, destruction, and suffering that lay in the wake of the Civil War, World Wars I and II, the Korean War, Vietnam, Afghanistan, and the Gulf War. **Our politics focus on winning the *war* on poverty, drugs, crime, and terrorism instead of looking at these ills and the threats they pose as the symptoms of an ill society that generates so much death and destruction and continues to justify it as abusers do in their individual families.** There is no way to accurately assess the suffering of the most overt wars or to assess the suffering of crushing poverty, hatred of minorities, inhumane working conditions, and rampant injustice. We can only begin to understand the cost by understanding that all these wars, large and small, are our symptoms—the Cry for Help for America. **War is a symptom of Low-Tech Human Relations.** The antidote to war is peace. That is the Case for Peace, for the hard work it takes to make peace, and we know now that what it takes is a commitment to Repair with one another and to rework our relationship to power from power-over to power-with.

Many couples come to therapy dead set on having the therapist pass judgment on who is right and who is wrong. And while there are dysfunctional or even abusive behaviors that need to be identified and worked with (of course), the goal is always loving, safe reconnection (or safe disconnection if need be). The goal is never war. It would not have served Pam and her husband to debate who was more entitled to be angry. What served them was for Pam to work through a wound that was preventing her from coming back to the table to work things out after conflict. What served them as a couple was whatever it took to get back on the road to each other. Yet these same values are not on the political agenda here in America and not spoken of in political platforms or debates, as all the mockery of Marianne Williamson illustrates so well and so sadly for America. The fact that peace is not a goal for our country is both horrifying and highly diagnostic, just as it is for a warring family, where lack of intervention causes unending pain and is potentially lethal. The fact that safety, peace, and love are not our goals *is America's Cry for Help*.

A Focus on the Common Good

The focus of family therapy is on *the common good*, which creates peace for everyone. The Case for Peace I am talking about for America is the peace that is born of us *taking a stand together for our common good—* that means all of us, everyone in the Family of America. If you are not safe, then I am not safe either.

Peace is an urgent evolutionary challenge. We have evolved in so many miraculous ways. Our thinking and tool-making capacities have evolved like no other life form here on earth. I recently watched a documentary on the Mars Rovers, where two robots, Opportunity and Spirit (appropriately named), were sent to Mars to explore its surface and see if there might have been water there at one time that could have supported life. The technology that built the robots and successfully got them there was astounding, beyond imagination for a right-brained person like me, a true testimony to human intelligence, creativity, and skill. But our next evolutionary challenge is not a technological issue. It is an issue of using all that brain power to explore and rework our internal wiring—our psychology that is not functioning properly—so that we may survive amidst the many advances we have made, some of which now put all our lives at risk.

I believe the Case for Peace is our only option if we want to survive. I am saying again that peace is not, in essence, a political, ideological, or even a moral issue. It can be construed in all those ways, but peace for America and for humanity today *is the difference between life and death for us*. War is still on the table because we are under the spell of abuse dynamics in our homes and in the national political arena. The trance of abuse is held in place by a fierce belief in and desire to maintain power-over others, in domination and forced submission.

Many wars have, in fact, resulted in periods of peace—for a while. In personal relationships and national and international relationships, we can only sustain outright aggression for so long before a truce is called or one side is forced to concede, surrenders, or is destroyed. After war, cultures may be rebuilt, governments reformed and redesigned, and populations renewed, but it is only a matter of time before another war starts somewhere else. This is because the underlying psychological dynamic of domination and subjugation of others to get our perceived wants met has not changed.

Human beings have survived for untold thousands of years by both cooperating and competing with one another, and that worked well enough, especially for those who have competed the most successfully. But our world has changed. We now must recognize that we have competed ourselves into a corner by competing globally for the biggest, deadliest weapons, the most territory we can snatch from others, the biggest bank accounts, and the most righteousness, influence, and control. Why do we have to face this? Because the number one way we try to get more of all these things today is by killing more people! We are killing each other every day. According to the United Nations, over fifteen hundred children have been killed or injured in Russia's war on Ukraine (acknowledging that the real numbers may be much higher), most caused by explosive weapons that have a wide range of destruction.[52] In other reports, it is estimated that, as of August 27, 2023, there have been over nine thousand civilian deaths, over seventeen thousand injured in Ukraine, and up to five hundred thousand military casualties on both sides.[53, 54] These are not just statistics—they are people like you and me who had homes, jobs, and loved ones and who had aspirations and dreams for their lives. And this is just one small slice of the casualties of war around the globe. The United States continues to send millions in military assistance to Ukrainians. I do understand that the desire to come to the aid of a nation under attack can seem the same as coming to the aid of an abused child or spouse because thousands of lives are at stake. At the same time, could the toll of such needless death and destruction—with no end in sight—be the alarm bell that wakes us up to the futility of war itself—that wakes us up to commit our billions to world peace?

We are the only animal that has gotten itself, *by our own behaviors*, out of balance with the entire natural world. Uncontrolled competition with each other and unrestrained domination of nature have put us at the top of nearly every food chain, except, perhaps, for the viral and bacterial worlds. We have a choice now about whether we are willing or not to accept the fact that we simply cannot survive without changing our relationship to the natural world. **But what most of us do not realize, which is the single most important reason I am writing this book, is that we cannot survive without changing our relationship to ourselves.** If we do not blow each other up, and if global warming or a natural catastrophe does not wipe us out in the very near future, the human race may persist as an animal for some time to come, but as we gobble up the life force energy of one another in a mad race for dominance, we may not have killed off our food source entirely, but we will have killed off what makes us most human—love, care, connection, cooperation, and a *conscience, a sense of right and wrong that informs how we relate to others and alerts us to our impact on them.* When we change our relationship to one another, when we shift from abuse dynamics to High-Tech Human Relations, our relationship to the natural world will solve itself. When the survival of all humanity is our objective, we will not want to poison the air, water, and soil we depend on to stay alive.

Shifting from a power-over to a power-with paradigm does not mean that there is no place for competition. Human beings are competitive by nature, and the urge to compare and compete has us strive to accomplish more and do better all the time. Scientists compete to come up with the best cures, and computer wizards compete to devise better apps and more efficient programs. But the evolutionary challenge that ensures that safety and peace are priorities is that we compete *within a container of cooperation,* like a well-functioning family. **In other words, the most appropriate and sustainable place for competition is within a context of what serves the viability of the whole group, nation, and, ultimately, the whole family of humankind.** A good word for this is sovereign unity. We are sovereign within our own domains to think, feel, and behave, to compete, grow, and achieve with whatever talents or callings we have— *within the context of what is safe and peaceful for everyone.* This is how we would describe a healthy family. Sovereign unity implies a powerful balance between self and other. We are sovereign, and we are united, and we commit to working together and settling conflict without violence to maintain that balance to the very best of our ability. These are the deeper cuts of High-Tech Human Relations. The looming possibility of our extinction calls us to evolve our consciousness through the repair of our collective mental health.

This is it! I tell America. *We don't need a diagnostic manual to explain the dangerous state of mind that is running too much of the show here at home and around the world. We know that war is all around.*

War, an extreme power-over model of human functioning, is the mindset of the *premeditated murder* of people. We humans have been listening to our animalistic instincts and doing whatever it takes to be predators and not prey for most of known history. The predator and prey dynamic is one of power-over; one eats, and the other is eaten. It is a revolutionary and evolutionary challenge to change our human operating system to one of power that is shared for the common good. The conditions we have created are calling us to evolve our consciousness to this new psychological maturity. We are being asked to make a dizzying 180-degree shift away from all the imbalances of power that have led to massive abuse and injustice. Psychological maturity means your needs, your views, your beliefs, and your models of behavior are as important as mine and deserve to be heard and respected as much as mine do. *And none of us has the right to impose any of that on others against their will* (again—unless we are talking about restraining those who pose a threat to the lives and safety of others or themselves).

It's a nice theory, America says with some doubt in her voice. *But it sounds extremely difficult to enact.*

I know, I tell her. *Those invested in power-over are quick to label any approach to human relations based on mutual care as socialism or communism. They make it an ideological and political issue when, really, it is an issue not only of mental health but of our survival.*

The Case for Peace is Hard Work

Yes, I know the Case for Peace is revolutionary beyond what many of us can imagine or believe possible. (And there are many for whom the idea of shifting to a power-with world is not even desirable.) There is no question that it is hard work. It would require huge amounts of time at the bargaining table, and it would likely bring up more questions than answers once we get started: How do we share water rights? What do we allow to be put into our soil? How much of the expenses of medical care and education should be covered by the collective? What do we do with people who are violent? How do we respond to aggressive nations? And on and on and on. It would be hard work, endlessly hard, perhaps, but imagine a nation in which we commit to that hard work, where we sit at the table together for as long as it takes until we have an agreement everyone can live with, where no one is overpowered, vilified, or tear-gassed, where everyone has a voice, and the best possible consensus is reached because consensus and peaceful conflict resolution are what will bring us back together. When we look at the work involved in the Case for Peace, we must ask ourselves, how hard is the work of war? How hard is the work of rebuilding bombed-out cities, of a whole population adjusting to domination by a foreign power, and of rebuilding the shattered homes, bodies, and countless broken hearts of fatherless or motherless children, widows or widowers, or a lost generation of elders?

Understanding and agreement are not impossible, and they don't have to cost us a single life. The tug-of-war that results from the power-over paradigm and the win/lose model of relating it perpetuates—creates—polarization, us against them. It reinforces a hierarchical power structure of human relations that has the potential to oppress (and most often does oppress) those at the bottom of the hierarchy. It intensifies the perpetrator and victim cycle. All these outcomes of a power-over—a domination and suppression model of human relations—are what make lasting peace impossible. In couples therapy, neither partner is treated as less than or superior to the other. Therapy creates the context in which they come to the table of Repair as equals.

The logical, if not highly confronting, conclusion about a shift from a power-over to a power-with model of human relations is that we begin to know ourselves—all human beings—as equals.

Equality: The Last Frontier?

It is an odd profession being a psychotherapist. It's like being in a graduate program in human relations that no one ever graduates from. We learn enough of the basics to get a degree, and then we are thrown into the complex arena of human nature, human nurture, and human suffering. As psychotherapists, we learn a new dance every day, never the same step twice, because no two clients are the same. The work of psychology is not like building a house or repairing a leaky pipe. Yes, we carry our tool bags, too, but *we ourselves are also the hammer and the wrench, the nail and the fitting*, and that is daunting, to say the least. There may be therapists who do not agree, who are experts in a particular style or method of therapy, who use their skills like the best surgeons extracting a tumor or a bursting appendix. But I am not one of them, and I would have to say that role is neither desirable nor attainable for me. No matter what the presenting issue, a fundamental of psychotherapy is that we are reworking our injured relationships with other people and ourselves. How do we do that *without* experiencing a new and different relationship with another human being as part of the process?

It is an odd profession being a psychotherapist because, despite the relational dynamic, it is still one-sided. The new relationship we forge with a therapist is not like having a new friend or lover, and yet it is also not exactly like going to a car mechanic or handing authority to any other expert. If we are rebuilding a damaged foundation in human relationship, that foundation cannot be built on a one-up dynamic. One-up is not Repair. One-up is likely what injured us in the first place. At the very same time, as therapists, we are trained to not talk about ourselves, to hold that boundary, and to keep the focus on our clients. I have no argument with this in a general way. No one comes to therapy to hear about my childhood or my marriage. But without telling our stories, I believe we must convey that we have stories, too, and that we continue to learn and grow. I believe there is a felt relational edge we walk with our clients, a sense of shared humanity. I call this equality. We are equals. I have a different role from you, but I am not above you. I am your equal.

Adam and I had been working together for some time on his relationship issues. One day, he brought up an argument he just had with his partner, how they triggered each other, and how the level of upset they both felt often seemed out of proportion to the actual issues. Adam looked at me somewhat sheepishly and said, "You and your husband probably don't have these issues." Meaning you, being a therapist, must have it all figured out by now. You and your husband probably have a perfect relationship. In his imagination, Adam already saw himself as less-than, trailing far behind me in the race to have the best relationship. And, of course, it wasn't true that my husband and I were above the human fray. But suddenly, the Dance of Power had changed. Adam was unconsciously (and quite understandably) giving me a power that would not serve him. How did I adjust my own steps in that precarious moment and not unconsciously follow Adam's lead? "No," I said, "relationship is a process of rupture and repair. We all have ruptures. We all need to do the work of repair." The point is not that there will be no conflict between people because that is not possible. The point is that we are learning to Repair, that we are committed to coming back to love and connection, and my husband and I work on this, too. We try to ride the bike of our relationship with more balance and stability, but we all fall off, and falling is not failure. There is no failure. Success is getting back on the bike.

Equality is a delicate issue. I may have an experience or understanding you don't have, but I am not better than you. How do I communicate that without you idealizing me and without you giving too big a chunk of your power to me? I won't tell you my story, but I must find a way to let you know I've fallen off my bike too many times to count. Otherwise, therapy does not fully embody a new and healing relationship.

I didn't learn any of this before I started practicing, and I doubt I've always communicated this well. I learned it in the trenches. I learned it when I said something that felt hurtful to a client, and I needed to take responsibility and apologize. I learned it by having a therapist who couldn't do that for me. I learned it going home from what felt like the best session in the world and then getting triggered when my husband didn't ask me about my day after we spent a half hour talking about his. I am still learning. We are equals—in our worthiness, our vulnerabilities, our imperfections, and in our strengths and gifts. In our humanness. If only we could see this and embrace this as Americans, as a country, and as world citizens.

When we know ourselves as equals, it will make sense that safety and peace serve both the individual and the collective at the same time, and power is best directed toward the common good when it is shared, not lorded over anyone, whether in a family or in a nation. **What we don't** often understand, but which psychology today makes conscious for us, is that power can only be truly shared when we know ourselves as equals. Therefore, true peace rests on an acceptance of our equal value and deservedness. This, I imagine, will not go down easily for many in America today. I tried to warn you, dear reader, that as we dive deeper into what High-Tech Human Relations are all about, we will see that our operating system as individuals and as a nation is terribly outdated and urgently needs to be taken apart and reassembled.

What is a Culture of Equality?

A culture of equality is one in which we believe that all people have equal value, deserve equal consideration, and have equal rights. In a nutshell, a culture of equality means we all deserve to be treated with High-Tech Human Relations. We are all equally entitled to love, inclusion, and provision of our basic needs for survival. We all deserve to have our boundaries respected, our differences tolerated and accepted, and be met in our conflicts with a commitment to peaceful resolution. **Equality means we strive to treat others exactly the way we ourselves want to be treated and that no one is either more or less entitled.**

Equality does not mean we will all have the same income or opportunities. I am not talking about some form of socialism or any political ideology. I am talking only about how we treat one another, whatever our circumstances may be. Equality does not eliminate personal authority or end all hierarchy. We will still decide how our businesses are run, and we will continue to tell our employees what to do. We will still tell our children when to go to bed. Schools will continue to make rules for classroom behavior, and governments will still pass laws. But in a climate of equality, our personal authority and the authority of any group or governing body are held together within a context of care and respect for *everyone's* well-being in a context of dialogue and openness to many points of view and with the goal of meeting as many of our legitimate needs as possible. This doesn't mean a parent has to have a long dialogue about bedtime with a two-year-old, but it also doesn't mean we throw our power around because we are bigger and stronger. And just to repeat—we won't do it perfectly, but we can learn from our missteps; we can learn to be accountable, to come back to the table and repair whatever ruptures we have created and whatever damage we have done.

The one-up dynamics created and reinforced by abuse and the perpetuation of a perpetrator and victim mentality with all the imbalances of power that it operates on are what keep us from feeling like equals, knowing ourselves as equals, and acting toward others like equals. And this is exactly what abusive individuals and governments want. They want a system of power-over, and they need it to remain in power.

What is evolutionary about the idea of equality is that it requires us to fulfill our responsibilities and roles (whether we are parents or CEOs or the President of the United States) *without* violating the rights of others or harming them and with an attitude and an approach that is healing for everyone. That is the attitude and approach of High-Tech Human Relations—with love and care, with inclusion and tolerance of diversity, and with cooperation and nonviolent communication. We might have to put someone in handcuffs for everyone's safety, but we will know there is a victim somewhere inside them who has not been helped and has become a perpetrator, and we will do our best to help them now, even behind bars if need be. We will look for the underlying humanity in everyone, and we will do our best to treat each other as *equal in value* to ourselves, even if it means restraining them.

I think we all know how difficult this can be to do. Yet, if you have ever had the experience of another listening to you as an equal, as worthy of respect even when you disagree, are angry, or have hurt feelings, you know that it is one of the best experiences you can have with another person. The fight goes out of you. You are at *peace* and open to Repair, and you want to do the same for them. If you have not had this experience, can you imagine how wonderful it would be to *not* meet a wall of resistance, defense, blame, or dismissal from another? I try to imagine that nonviolent communication rooted in a shared sense of power and a deep recognition of our equal value as human beings could be what we witness in political discourse and how different our country would be if we role-modeled this for each other and all our children—as teachers, workers, as law enforcement and government officials, and as president. I try to imagine a group of senators and representatives standing up and calling out verbal abuse on the floors of Congress. I try to imagine them in their participation in the media, calling out talk of violence and blatant lies coming from their colleagues—in a spirit of power-with and in a spirit of calling them to remember the oaths they took, the broad and diverse spectrum of humanity they represent and are supposed to be a voice for, and in a spirit of calling them to the table of adult, peaceful, negotiation and Repair. And I try to imagine them doing this again and again, however long it takes and however much resistance and criticism they receive, embodying a mature approach to opposition and a model for Repair and reconnection with one another for the good of the country. For the good of everyone equally.

I try to imagine that there is a position in government specifically designed to mediate congressional disagreements, roadblocks, and hostilities. In November of 2021, CNN reported that Republican Representative Paul Gosar had posted an animated video that appeared to show him killing Democratic Representative Alexandria Ocasio-Cortez and going after President Biden with swords.[55] In The Guardian, it was reported that there was a great outcry, especially among Democrats, and Gosar was censured and stripped of a committee position. These would be actions I would call restraint, and rightfully so. Those calling out Gosar's video argued that posting violence and violent rhetoric from elected officials can urge people to actual violence, using the insurrection at the US Capitol as a glaring example. "We cannot dismiss Representative Gosar's violent fantasies as a joke because in this decade, in this America, someone's going to take him seriously," said Congresswoman Mary Gay Scanlon.[56] And they did. And they do.

I try to imagine that a trained mediator called Gosar to a meeting with Ocasio-Cortez and told them both that the purpose of the meeting was to create a space of safety for them both to listen and be heard, with the hope that they could leave the meeting with a new understanding of one another. In my imagination, Gosar was asked to listen to and take in the impact the video had on Ocasio-Cortez and was given the opportunity to voice his issues with her in exactly the way he would want another person to voice their complaints about him—what he thought and felt, and what would help him know he was heard even if they didn't agree. In my mind's eye, I saw the facilitator stopping him firmly but respectfully if he continued the attack, but I prefer to imagine he got it, that he backed down and acknowledged that he would not want anyone to post such a video about him or someone he loves and that he began to see he is entitled to his feelings and his views but not to his threatening behavior. I prefer to imagine that he understood that his video might well have been taken seriously by any number of mentally ill supporters. I imagined the facilitator asking him if he or anyone he loved had ever been attacked or under threat. What had his parents and family role-modeled for him about relationships? What had he learned in the past, and what did he believe was expected of him in the present about how to deal with conflict? Where, perhaps, was the victim in him that had identified with the aggressor? Then, I imagined the facilitator giving Ocasio-Cortez the same space to be heard, her feelings validated, the abuse depicted on the video acknowledged, and I imagined she was supported to talk about the lasting effects without being shamed for declaring that she had been victimized. I see her being encouraged to share how feelings of threat and unsafety might have related to anything in her history that was similar. And then,

I imagine she was given the opportunity to ask for everything she needed from Gosar to feel heard and safe and that he was asked to respond. I like to think this meeting made the news, not as shame and blame of Gosar but as an example of how our government can be committed to safety and peaceful conflict resolution even in the face of fierce disagreement within the family of the government and as a model for our children, our country, and the world.

We can all learn to do this for each other because we are already learning to do it in the best therapy settings, mediation, and other models of peaceful conflict resolution. And many of us are learning to do it in our ordinary lives. It is not as complicated or as difficult as it might sound, but it requires a total shift in our collective beliefs about the value of every human being. I am talking about bringing an attitude of compassion, empathy, understanding, and goodwill to others, along with healthy boundaries **and a desire to see others heal and thrive because they matter as much as I matter, and their welfare is as important as mine.**

My husband and I went out to dinner recently with my daughter. Our waitress was clearly upset about something and was noticeably short with us. Rather than be annoyed or complain to the manager, my daughter talked to the waitress with great kindness. She asked her if she was having a hard day and if there was anything we could do. The waitress literally transformed at that moment—her posture softened, she made eye contact with us, and she was lovely for the rest of the evening. We never found out what was bothering her, but it didn't matter. What mattered was that her welfare as the one serving us was as important as our welfare as the ones being served. I imagine that moment of compassion changed her entire night, and maybe she went home to her partner or children relaxed and open rather than upset and closed off. That one moment could very likely have created a ripple effect of peace and safety for a whole family. That's the power we have when we use our power for the benefit of the whole.

One small but caring moment in one encounter—it cost nothing, and it was priceless! We can do this for each other. There are over three hundred million people here in America. What an amazing step toward peace we could create at home and in the world with just one moment of connection and compassion with one other person every day. We don't have to be therapists, mediators, educated, or rich to change our step in the dance we do with others. When your well-being is *equal in value* to mine, we have the evolution of consciousness toward High-Tech Human Relations in action, and we have the possibility of peace. Many of us already do this, and there are many more of us badly in need of receiving these simple acts of caring. There are many people who have never experienced caring. We meet them in our therapy offices more often than you might imagine. James, the man who imagined me as a protective tiger, was one of those people. He had never received a loving touch or a word of kindness or praise growing up. He was ignored, assaulted, and violated, but by some miracle, he was still alive and functioning enough to get by— barely. Someone just like James might be our waiter the next time we eat out—how would we like to be with him, and what can we do to help him bring safety and peace back to his family when he goes home?

Peace is a complex concept. On the surface, it means no more war, but we know now that it requires a total shift in our way of being with one another. Peace is not static. It is a process that must be continually renewed with practices, policies, and structures to maintain it, like the six elements of Repair, like embodying a totally new way of exercising power *with* one another and embracing a psychology of peace and a recognition of the equal value of every human life. When it becomes a commonly held commitment that I will not treat you in any way that I do not want to be treated, there will be no more rape and pillaging, no more destruction of the environment to create wealth for a few at the expense of the many, and no more political, sexual, religious, or economic tyranny. When we all understand that your welfare is just as important as mine—

your children, your body, your home, and your beliefs are as sacred as mine—we will be evolving into the next level of consciousness that is required for humanity to survive. We have come to a fork in the road where the extremes of domination and submission are *no longer sustainable*; they are the dinosaur we ourselves are tasked with making extinct. I am not talking about an ideology or a political position. This is not Left or Right. It is not feminism or a religion. **Safety, peace, love, shared power, and equality are the lifeboat we need to build and get on together. They are the rescue from our sinking vessel.**

It will take all our strength to hold back the tidal wave of national and individual abusive family dynamics that are pushing our boat under. The reward for all the hard work of committing to peace and maintaining it is the joy of peace itself!

We know how to harness water, wind, and the sun's rays to generate the energy needed for our most demanding machinery and equipment. Our evolutionary challenge is to harness all the energy trapped in greed, judgment, rage, intolerance, and aggression—and use it to power the machinery of High-Tech Human Relations. Unharnessed, we have explosions of rage, hatred, self-harm, and violence toward others. These unharnessed emotions and the Low-Tech Human Relations and dynamics of abuse they fuel and empower can be converted into all the energy we need for a safe and peaceful world. This is a limitless source of sustainable, renewable energy.

You see, I tell America, *this is what we do in the best therapy. Through a healing relationship with a safe person, we can unearth and release the energies inside us that have gotten trapped in blame, shame, anger, fear, and judgment. These energies then become available to sustain us and grow our greatest potentials. What if we lead the way to peaceful conflict resolution here and abroad? What if we were the ones?!*

I know what America in Therapy means now, America says, her torch flickering just slightly. *It means we become the safe harbor for one other.*

We make it safe. We create peace. We build the lifeboat and reach out our hands to one person at a time. We help everyone get out from under the riptide of abuse and take us all to shore.

Good, I tell her. *Then you're ready for Love now.*

Chapter 12:

THE CASE FOR LOVE

Curiously and frighteningly, love has been excommunicated from political discourse, from the highest level of conversation in the Family of America. It may be easier to talk about love on the personal level, the love we didn't get, and the love we have a hard time giving. On the political front, love is still seen as a weakness, a liability, the talk of "girls" and sissies. It is mocked and dismissed, just as Marianne Williamson was mocked and dismissed. Yet love is what we all seem to want most—love, care, kindness, and consideration. I have never had a single client who came to therapy to fortify their defenses, learn to fight more aggressively, or wall others out more effectively. People come to therapy to heal those injuries and experience more love, belonging, and safe, satisfying relationship in their lives. In our personal lives and in our families, we do not consider love a weakness. We crave it. In all the years I have been a therapist, I have not met one person whose deepest wounds did not come from an injury to love. We spend years in painful relationships and struggle with addiction, loneliness, depression, anxiety, and endless forms of failure to thrive, all because love was missing, lost, betrayed, or violated at some critical time with critically important people. Even so, the love we seem to value most in our personal lives is not a political priority; it is not even a consideration. Why might this be so? Is it because peace advocates won't mobilize the troops? Women won't push the button? Yes! A commitment to love and connection would make it nearly *impossible* to wage war and out of the question to launch nuclear missiles. And that is exactly what we need!

As a nation, it is long past time we confront the massive disconnect between the love, safety, and peace we all crave (and the suffering we experience to the extent we don't have these things) and what we legislate and believe in as national policy and practice. And while, as I said, it is not within the scope of this book to examine patriarchy and feminism in depth, I do believe we must confront, as a nation, all the ways we have relegated what we consider the feminine impulses and qualities of love, nurturance, and connection to a realm *outside* politics. Without understanding our desperate need to embody these qualities as a nation and incorporate them into our thinking, our rhetoric, our platforms, and our policies, we are perpetuating the dynamics of abuse in our country from the top down and the bottom up.

Our whole conversation must change if we are to get out of this death-trap. Like peace, love is not a weakness, as abusive adults and abusive governments would have us believe. **Love is the healthiest sustenance for human beings.** We know that plants don't thrive in a dark, mineral-poor environment or without water. It would be absurd if we blamed the plant that failed to grow and blossom in such conditions and claimed it didn't try hard enough or was lazy or worthless. Yet this is exactly how we treat so many people here in America. We deprive them of love, care, safety, and the necessities of life, and when they don't live up to the

"American Dream," we allow ourselves to believe they are bad, inferior people and should be punished or wiped out. This makes no psychological sense, yet as a nation, we have not caught up politically with all that has been learned from the millions of hours we spend as psychotherapists treating people in pain, people who have tried their best to grow in the dark and without enough water and who have not quite made it. Can we understand that when we fail to provide the highest level of human relations, High-Tech Human Relations, to all human beings, we ourselves become as unhealthy as a flower kept in the dark? Can we also understand that there is a huge difference between a flower deprived of sunlight and a human being deprived of love, care, and connection? The flower wilts and dies and quietly returns to dust. Human beings deprived of love and connection are not likely to quietly disappear. They *act out and act in*— turn against others or self or both—in ways that today are increasingly lethal to large numbers of people and other life forms. We can no longer allow ourselves to summarily conclude that the most symptomatic among us are flawed by nature, lazy, inferior, or born evil. We can no longer justify condemning them and throwing them away because we, as a society, are failing to provide the conditions they need to grow. We must look at the environment we are providing for one another, identify what is toxic and remove it, and identify what is healthy and supply it!

Think of a time, dear reader, when you felt disconnected, unwanted, betrayed, unvalued, or violated. No one *wants* more of that. Hatred is indigestible and makes us sick. Feeding ourselves and those around us hatred, intolerance, violence, and abuse is like feeding ourselves and our children rotten food on a continuum to feeding them cyanide. Now, think of a time you felt loved. Was it not the most blessed feeling? Warm and full, held and safe—a time you could breathe deep and relax all the tension and stress in your body and your being. Didn't you want more? Or maybe you haven't fully experienced that kind of love, but you know somewhere deep in your being that it is missing, and you long for it. Love is the best sustenance for human beings. It is the most important ingredient in High-Tech Human Relations. And why is this an issue of national concern? Because people who are loved and cared for do not want to exploit, attack, or kill others.

What we have learned is that human beings need a diet of safety, peace, and love to become the most caring, constructive, and contributing adults possible, for ourselves and for others. We must ask ourselves why we wouldn't want to provide that, why we don't fund it, why it isn't at the top of the list for national security, and why it isn't on the agenda for every political campaign and presidential debate. I'm afraid that one big answer to that question is that a politics of love is not profitable. I'm afraid love isn't a political priority because it would mean the end of power-over and the extremes of domination and submission that empower those at the top of the food chain. Love in politics would ask us to know ourselves as equals in value and equally worthy of consideration, care, and justice. What we really must do is educate ourselves about the *politics of abuse*—of scapegoating, blame, suppression, and aggression—so that we can understand the urgency to evolve our consciousness into the politics of love—of disarmament, inclusion, provision, caring, and peace. I'm afraid too many become extraordinarily rich and powerful from the politics of abuse, and they most likely will not want us to be educated in these ways. They certainly don't want me to be having this conversation with you. This is the reason abusive governments persecute journalists, peaceful protesters, and truth-tellers, ban their books, and portray them as enemies of the people. **The psychology of abuse does everything in its power to stamp out the psychology of love.** Conflict, war on all levels, discrimination, the unrestrained widening gap between the rich and the poor, and the culture of incarceration are some of its most effective psychological weapons.

A publication called Literacy Mid-South reported that correctional professionals found there is a connection between poor literacy, drop-out rates, and criminal behavior. Their data showed that 70% of all jailed adults could not read at a fourth-grade level, "meaning they lack the reading skills to navigate many everyday tasks or hold down anything but lower (paying) jobs." And they found that those without sufficient income from employment are the most prone to crime.[57] It's not rocket science to see what a politics of love would do. We would take on, as a country, the responsibility of making sure all our children are well educated as a priority, and we would acknowledge that our failure to invest in the success of every child has provided the perfect funnel into our prison system and the free labor (slave) it provides. In an article published by the Corporate Accountability Lab in 2020, it was reported that *prison labor* is an important part of the prison system in America. "Private corporations are incentivized to lobby for policies that maximize prison populations in order to sustain a business model that is only profitable because they can exploit artificially deflated labor costs." It was reported that more than forty-one hundred corporations profit from mass incarceration in our country, some of which are the private prisons themselves that have lucrative government contracts that include minimum bed guarantees and a fixed price per prisoner! The article further states that the incentive to provide cheap prison labor works against the whole notion of prison reform.[58] Why reform a system that has the prison industry itself and many corporations *profit* from injustice?

These are dynamics of abuse operating at high levels. People who are already deprived, who statistically have a much greater likelihood of being incarcerated, find themselves trapped in a situation where they can be exploited again.

These are abuse family dynamics on a national scale, I tell America.

In addition to low literacy rates, the data also shows that people who were abused in childhood also have much higher rates of imprisonment. The Compassion Project published these findings: 63% of incarcerated men had a history of emotional abuse, 60% had suffered physical abuse, and 49% had been sexually abused. These numbers are double to triple the rates of non-incarcerated men. For incarcerated women, the statistics were similar: 59% had been emotionally abused, 54% had been physically abused, and 52% had been sexually abused. All much higher rates in comparison to non-incarcerated women.[59]

This means people who have been abused are at *higher risk* for incarceration and, thus, for being victimized yet again by a national system that is not committed to providing the necessities of life for all people. I don't want to get wrapped up in endless statistics. I want to talk about love. But most people don't know the sad connection between deprivation, crime, and incarceration and how profitable it is to ignore it. Too many politicians are quick to talk of criminals and thugs as if these people are a whole separate category of monsters. **But, in fact, we are blaming and punishing our victims instead of helping them. A politics of love would address poverty, racial injustice, housing and education issues, family violence, drug addiction, and a whole host of other ills before it would put one more person into prison slavery.**

I want to tell you a story, I tell America.

I had lunch one day with a man who worked for a big health insurance company. He was a numbers cruncher—his job was to figure out profit and loss for the insurance business. Naively, I said, "I love my clients." His response was, "That's why insurance companies hate master's level therapists! You love your clients too much!" Meaning—you work with them too long. You cost us too much money. In that moment, I understood why the business of healthcare and the actual work of mental health seemed to be worlds apart.

I wondered if he had ever been to therapy himself or if he ever suffered pain he didn't know how to deal with. Or was he too frightened to ask for help? I wondered how much love might have been missing from his life that the need for it had become something to belittle. I was pretty sure he didn't have a clue what it is like to sit in a therapist's chair and hear tale after tale of ordinary people who were raped or locked in basements, the little girl who tried to hang herself when she was five, the little boy who saw his mother beaten and bloody. Or the stories of many more who came home every day to a father passed out on the living room floor, a mother immobilized by depression, parents who were raging and unavailable or who tormented them with shaming messages—you're too fat, too thin, too stupid, too emotional—or parents who said they wished the child had never been born or threatened to return them to the adoption agency. I wondered if he ever thought about how many of those who cannot afford help repeat what was done to them, hurt their children, sabotage their jobs, or end up in jail.

If we are not allowed to love each other back to health in the places where the deepest wound is lack of love in one form or another, what do we imagine heals? Loving our clients is not all there is to psychotherapy—of course not. But if we don't love our clients, what do we imagine psychotherapy is going to do for them? If we don't hold love and care for the innocent, precious being that was born into their infant body and was later covered over by layers of hurtful conditioning, what do we think will help them reconnect to that essence and to love in themselves? A technique? A pep talk? A buck up and move on conversation? Loss of love is the greatest wound we can suffer. In the world of psychology, we know that love in some form and in some relationship is an essential part of healing.

The injury to our psyches comes from internalizing negative, unloving messages about who we are *from other people*. Therefore, part of the job of psychotherapy is to help people discover and internalize the positive messages they did not get or did not get enough of early on. This is key to forming healthy relationships, coping with stress constructively, and finding fulfillment in creativity, work, and play. We therapists cannot adequately do that job if, in the very intimate setting where clients bare their deepest vulnerabilities, they are not internalizing love and care from us in some form.

We are Wired for Love

We come into this world wired for love. An article from *Psych Care: Psychology Services LLC* references some of the leading authorities on what we know about love, connection, and our mental health. Abraham Maslow, a well-known American psychologist, identifies love and belonging as right up there in importance for human survival as oxygen, food, water, shelter, sleep, and physical safety. Neuroscientist Dr. Matthew Lieberman, director of UCLA's Social Cognitive Neuroscience lab, states that our need for connection with others is even more critical than food and shelter and is the primary motivation behind human behavior. Dr. Brene Brown, well-known for her research on human connection, tells us that for infants, connection is survival, but as we grow up, our needs for connection become more complex and include the need to thrive emotionally, physically, spiritually, and intellectually.[60]

Good psychotherapy is one powerful way to help repair and reconnect the wires within us that have been damaged or disconnected from mistreatment by other human beings who, for many of the reasons we have explored throughout this book, are operating with very damaged and broken wiring themselves. Abuse is what unplugs that wiring and makes it possible for us to hurt ourselves and one another without feeling the necessary empathy or remorse to bring ourselves off the ledge of division and violence. Abuse is both a symptom and a cause of the broken bonds of love between parent and child. I say this to raise an alarm. Parents are not supposed to burn their children, lock them in basements, or abandon them. We are not wired this way, but we are doing these things, and it is not just someone else who does this. The people I have seen in my practice who have suffered these abuses and torture are you and me. They work, have friends, are creative, get up in the morning and brush their teeth, make breakfast, and walk their dogs. But they too often grew up with parents who did not love them, were not bonded to them, and hurt them beyond what imagination can sometimes conjure up. Their stories are the stuff of nightmares and horror movies. And they suffer in ways many of us don't know and can't comprehend unless we have been there ourselves. And I mean *suffer*—sleeplessness, debilitating depression, uncontrollable rages, self-harm, massive anxiety, painful relationships, agonizing loneliness, addiction, job loss, and suicidal ideation. The fact that they survived at all is a testimony to the tenacity of the human spirit and unshakable resilience.

The actual statistics on child abuse in America from a 2020 report by the American Society for the Positive Care of Children are horrifying. There were 7.1 million reports of child abuse. It was estimated that 1750 children died from abuse and neglect, 80.6% at the hands of at least one parent, and 46.4% under one year of age. The report went on to give statistics on physical and sexual abuse of children, child trafficking, and how many children were put into foster care. It was also reported that children who are abused and neglected are nine times more likely to be involved in criminal activity.[61] It is frightening to think how many of these children (to say nothing of abused adults as well) will not get help. And it is heartbreaking to imagine who they might have become if their parents and caregivers had been helped, if they had been rescued, and if their Cry for Help, individually and collectively, had been heard—and prioritized!

If any other species stopped caring for its young, the species would not survive. When humans do not care for their young, we may go on living in our bodies, but our minds and hearts become ill, *mentally ill*. Mental illness at the far end of the spectrum leads to suicide and homicide. When we stop caring for our young and assault, torture, and even kill them, it is inevitable that we create and intensify alienation, scapegoating, exploitation, and violence. These symptoms are the result of broken bonds of love, and untreated symptoms further break those bonds. Just as cancer destroys the body's ability to care for and heal itself, abusive individuals and institutions destroy our ability to work together for the common good. In America and in the world, if we don't find a way to come back to one another and unite for the good, we will be at the greatest risk of assaulting each other in ways we cannot recover from. For this reason, it is critical we learn how to come together to *break the cycle of abuse* and focus our efforts on prevention and healing rather than on blame and punishment.

A Spirit of Resilience

There are many people who have survived terrible childhoods and have not become frozen into submission or become abusive themselves. And there are many people who have healed from early abuse and trauma by finding healthy connection in other places. There are also cases we just can't explain about why or how certain people rise from the ashes of abuse and neglect and become radiant human beings. Like a man named Mully, featured in a documentary by that name, who was abandoned by his family and left homeless and destitute as a little boy in Kenya. From begging on the streets to becoming a multimillionaire, Charles Mully later committed his life and resources to rescuing and housing, adopting, feeding, and educating over twenty-six thousand orphaned Kenyan children like himself since 1989. Mully Children's Family now has six centers in Kenya.[62]

But for every Charles Mully, there are countless others who do not rise from the ashes without our help. What I have learned is that the very best hope for recovery for people who have been abused and neglected is to have one person who intervenes, one person who cares, who offers a safe harbor and reflects our essential goodness and worth and, if possible, can offer a road out of a life of violation and annihilation. One loving aunt who took her little niece for the summer, a neighbor who offered a couch when the violence at home was too much, a teacher who saw potential in a failing student and helped them apply for a scholarship, or a social worker, coach, or employer—anyone who reached out. We have the best chance of surviving abuse and neglect when someone outside the abusive system can offer love and care, connection and belonging, validation of our essential worth, and rescue or a path to safety. We have so many people like this in America today, mostly unsung heroes who don't make it to the news, people who volunteer in schools and work with children to develop empathy and end bullying, or those who volunteer in homeless shelters and food banks—all those supporting the most down and out among us instead of targeting them. These are the armies we want to fund. But again, I don't really want to use war terminology. These are the *revolutionaries* we need to pull us back from the brink of the mass psychological illness that threatens us.

Without an actual person to provide rescue or help, many people find healing connection in religion, in nature, with animals, or in creative pursuits. These connections are lifesavers for countless people. But I would have to add that, in my experience, the surest way to escape the cycle of abuse and heal is to find that loving connection *with people*. When the damage to our hearts, minds, and bodies has been inflicted by human hands, we need to have a reparative experience with others. That's what therapy is all about. The good news is that we can all learn how to become a safe connection for our fellow human beings.

No therapist, of course, is perfect. We are not the love saviors of the world. We are all healing our own wounds with the help of others, too. But we have an inside view of the healing power of love that many do not have, and we make that a conscious part of the work we do.

What do I mean by loving my clients? This is a very important question. I am not suggesting mushy feelings or bad boundaries. I'm talking about deeply caring that they have the best outcome *for themselves* from the work they do in therapy. Good therapists communicate this love by believing our clients' stories, feeling empathy for their pain, believing in their intrinsic worth, supporting their ability to tolerate difficult truths about themselves and others, and believing in their ability to heal and transform their lives into the best imperfect version of themselves they can envision. We hold that belief even when they can't. We do our very best not to judge them so they are safe to feel their most vulnerable feelings. We let them know that vulnerability is a strength and takes courage. We do our best to tolerate and work with the negative feelings or positive idealizations they may project onto us and not project our own wounds and needs onto them. It means, more than anything, we hold a space of love and care as a backdrop to any other intervention, technique, or process of therapy we use. We're rooting for our clients to get well!

Jackie was one of my very first clients. She was beaten mercilessly by her father. As a child, she was told, as so many abused children are, that he would beat her more if she didn't stop crying. She came to therapy because she had a new baby, and she was terrified by her desire to hit her tiny daughter when she cried. Fortunately, Jackie knew enough to seek help. It is frightening to imagine the outcome for Jackie and her baby if there was no one who could help her access *love* for the little girl in her who was not loved and whose vulnerability was cruelly violated by someone she was completely dependent on. There was nothing more important to do for Jackie than help her internalize the love she didn't get. This is the love she "borrows" and internalizes from the therapist and can take home to her baby. Judgment of her violent impulses would only shame her and would do nothing to heal the little girl who did not get love and did not know how to give it. Fortunately for Jackie, she had the awareness and the resources to get help. For all those who cannot find the love they didn't get, we must know the likely outcome is that they will be far more prone to snap at their babies' cries and reenact what was done to them. They might end up in prison, their baby in a hospital, and in any case, a whole new generation of pain and abuse would be born.

As a nation, we need to understand that our mental health issues are as serious and as life-threatening as any cancer or heart disease, may require as much or more treatment, and require as much or more attention and funding. The hope of this book is that our collective mental health can be understood in a much larger perspective than an insurance model, something we attribute to the marginalized and the poor, or a criminal justice issue. Jackie's story is a microcosmic snapshot of one of our greatest macrocosmic challenges. There are whole generations of violated, traumatized people here in America and around the world, some of whom, having little or no love, are carrying assault weapons and bombs, looking for innocent people *just like their tiny toddler selves* to reenact their traumas on, and some of them are running for office. This is the Terror of the Situation. The Hope for Our Country is that psychotherapy helps us understand what we need to do.

In the Case for Safety, I highlighted the absolute necessity of making the shift from power-over to power-with. In the Case for Peace, I highlighted the urgent need to expand that concept to include embracing and fostering our fundamental equality as human beings. In the Case for Love, I want to share with you the third big *Aha!* that came to me in my work as a therapist. I've referenced it earlier, but now I want to bring it center stage. As therapists and as ordinary human beings, one of the greatest gifts we can give one another, and one of the most healing messages of love we can convey, is that we see and speak to the essential nature of each one of us. We believe that inside every person is an essential self that was there before all the layers of conditioning distorted the ways we view ourselves and others. We reach through all that is stuck or blocked, hurt and violated, to connect to that essential self, and we don't give up.

Love is built on the belief in that essential goodness in all human beings, in our innate wiring for loving connection. There is no baby of any skin color, race, or sex born without it.

Ted was terribly abused as a child, abandoned by his father, and outcast by his mother, stepfather, and two stepbrothers. As an adult, Ted was an angry loner who had raged at his wife and child and eventually abandoned them. He came to therapy because he had just started a new relationship, and he was frightened of his anger and tendency to withdraw.

He told me that therapy was his very first experience of feeling there was anything in him worth salvaging. How we are seen by others has everything to do with how we relate to ourselves. Our essential selves can be *uncovered* by the love that sees through layers and layers of trauma and defense. This is not a fairy tale. It is not fantastical thinking. Ted worked hard both with the abuse he had suffered and the pain he had inflicted on others with his rage. He had a lot of amends to make, but we didn't start there. We started by building a lifeline of love that told him he was more than all he had done and all that had happened to him, and we made the connection between the two in a way that helped him move out of self-judgment, shame, and guilt. How did we do this? We went back into his childhood, the pain of his father leaving, the abuse that followed, and how he built up a wall of angry defense early on. We found his lonely little boy self who had given up on caring about or attaching to anyone— the little boy who *desperately wanted* to be cared for and belong safely to others. In this way, he found compassion for himself. This is the compassion love can bring to our frailties and our worst offenses. As a result, Ted discovered his own desire to make amends. He didn't have to be instructed, nor would that have been helpful in his specific case (though that can be helpful for others). The healing work he did with his child self impelled him quite naturally to repair his relationship with his son, and he eventually volunteered in a program for disadvantaged children. He was finally able to give the love he didn't get, and his new relationship was going well. Love was the essential ingredient that made it safe for him to face himself, be accountable, and change.

We don't have to be therapists to help others uncover their beautiful essence. In *Blaming the Victim*, the author, William Ryan, describes how he was assigned to teach a class of third-grade children in an inner-city school. He was told they were the slowest learners and not to expect much. Instead, he told them they were the brightest. He spoke to them as their essential selves, precious little beings waiting to be seen and affirmed, not through the lens of the projections and biases that had been placed on them. And they performed exactly as he had seen them, astounding an entire school system![63]

The fact that we have come to deny and repress the potential in so many of our fellow human beings reflects our national ill mental health. It is an abusive family dynamic in the Family of America that would label little third graders losers and, essentially, throw them away. It took so very little for William Ryan to do what he did with them. It cost nothing. He brought High-Tech Human Relations to a classroom of underprivileged children and likely changed their lives forever. There is nothing to say we can't do this for one another everywhere.

This is the same potential we can see in each other everywhere. While we need to give attention to the pain we have endured and the pain we have caused, we do that *as a passageway to freeing our strengths and gifts*—restoring our essential selves. Many people can't see their strengths, so we tell them right away—you survived. Isaac was adopted by parents who constantly threatened to send him back to an orphanage and told him no one else would ever want him. He had survived cancer, raised a foster child himself, and held down a good job. Isaac was literally shocked when I reflected to him what an amazing survivor he was. You made it through, I told him, and you made it here for help, regardless of all that came before. It took incredible strength to do that. The survivor in you not only endured but has hope for something better. We hold that for others, and they reclaim it as they reconnect to the essential selves they were to start with. We hold a belief in their strength and their power *for* them, like a light at the end of a tunnel they may not have believed they would ever find. Until they find it. We can all do this for one another.

We are talking about our human potential, which is our *national potential* as well. If there is an essential goodness in each one of us, and as America is made up of millions of individuals all with an essence waiting to be tapped into, acknowledged, and encouraged, then America has an essential goodness, too, that can be unearthed, fed, and grown. We have the power to either repress and deny the potential in all human beings, enslave and exploit them, or invite their greatest selves to the table. Whether we do this or not is a psychological issue that has become politicized.

In fact, we already do these things more than most of us may realize. The love that therapy exemplifies has always extended far beyond the scope of any specific form of treatment or intervention. There are countless individuals and programs here in America today that specifically help the most forgotten and targeted among us and that see the potential and the essential good in people and offer that reflection and a place for their light to shine and grow. They are the tip of a very big iceberg of love already alive and well in America. We hear about their efforts in our "human interest" stories or in "specials" on PBS. But I ask you, dear reader, to imagine how different our country would be if all the inspiring and heartfelt efforts at grassroots social reform were the bulk of the news we receive. I ask you to imagine how different our country would be if the raw footage of violence, division, and hatred were identified as the cancers we are here to treat and overcome; imagine how different our country would be if the essential selves inside Paul Gosar or the policeman who murdered George Floyd were the focus of what we speak to, try to help and heal as a role model of what is possible in addressing our great divides. It would be a different America. I think this is the core issue we must address—the climate of abuse that is polluting our human atmosphere and making so many of us sick.

I want to give you some examples of the kinds of love in action that we may not be aware of in America today. The Federal Bureau of Prisons published an article in March 2022 about their program of volunteerism in federal prisons. The volunteers offer a wide variety of services to help inmates, both while they are incarcerated and to help them make the transition back into society when they are released. They offer Alcoholics Anonymous, Narcotics Anonymous, trauma healing and crisis intervention, pet therapy, and physical activity. They teach life skills and foster connection through shared storytelling. They also offer an Alternative to Violence Program.[64] These volunteers are people who care and who want to make a difference in the lives of others. They are providing what the prison system does not.

You have it in you, I remind America. *You know what to do!*

Bryan Stevenson, Executive Director of the Equal Justice Initiative, is a man who has dedicated his life to helping and freeing incarcerated people who have been wrongly committed or unfairly sentenced. He's widely known for his book, *Just Mercy*, which was eventually turned into a feature film. Stevenson has this to say about humanity: "Every person is more than the worst thing they've ever done . . . If you take something that doesn't belong to you, you're not just a thief. Even if you kill someone, you're not just a killer. These are folks who have just been ignored and are desperate, hungry for someone to help them find a better way to cope."[65] This statement brings me easily to tears—**every person is more than the worst thing they have ever done.** Every person, somewhere inside, is the essential self they were at birth before anything happened to them, and people like Bryan Stevenson know that and reflect that back.

And he is not alone. AmeriCorps published an article in 2018 reporting that 77.34 million adults, 30.3 % of our population, volunteered through an organization the prior year, and we volunteered almost 6.9 billion hours at a value estimated to be $167 billion. Millions of people were supporting friends and family, and more than 51% were helping neighbors, illustrating that volunteerism and countless acts of goodwill are on the rise in America. Barbara Stewart, CEO of the Corporation for National and Community Service, was quoted as saying, "When we stand side-by-side to help others, our differences fade away, and we learn that Americans have more in common than we realize . . . We are changing lives and changing our communities through the power of care and connection with others who are hurting and in need."[66]

If America were *truly* in therapy, would we uncover this love of our fellow human beings as we peel back the layers of violence and hatred? Yes. There is no therapy, no real inner work, that uncovers a monster or a tyrant. The monsters and tyrants are a product of love lost and violated. The essential America is no different than the essential individual. What is America but a mass of individuals?

You see, hatred and violence bind us together with fear, submission, and rage, but those are not bonds—they are bondage, the same bondage found in abusive families, which consumes our life force and is too often deadly. Love is the umbilicus of life that holds us together in a life-giving and life-sustaining way. Love is the best healing for broken connection and the best access to healthy connection. Connection is the surest access to a sense of our shared humanity and cooperation for the common good. It is the road to peace and safety.

So, let's recount how operating from a place of love works on the broadest spectrum.

When we operate from love, we do not scapegoat or blame. We hold each other accountable while still seeing and speaking to the untouched essence in each of us. We hear the Cry for Help from the most symptomatic among us and try to uncover the causes of our pain and violence. We seek to heal rather than judge or punish. Love provides a safe passage from alienation to reconnection and Repair.

When we relate with love, we can embrace dependency and interdependency without shame and know our need for one another as a normal and necessary condition of being human. And we are safe to tell our stories and reveal our most difficult truths. When love is the foundation of our relationships, we do not lash out. We can transform our pain into appropriate power by taking responsibility, admitting fault, feeling remorse, and making amends.

When we prioritize love, we share power, resources, and opportunity. We do not take from others. We give. Because when we are grounded in love, we see all people as equally deserving of respect and care. From there, we seek the good of the whole in balance with the good of the individual. Then we know that true freedom comes when the oppression of abuse and violence is lifted and that true strength and power are found in our ability to love.

These are the attributes of High-Tech Human Relations. Love, in this context, is anything but weakness or passivity. It requires strength, perseverance, commitment, and courage.

America holds out her hands to me. She is crying. *Love does not martyr anyone,* she says. *Love is what has been martyred.*

I feel love awakening in America. I see it stirring, being released from the bonds of ignorance and pain that have imprisoned it for so long.

Love is demanding to be part of the conversation.

Chapter 13:

AMERICA THE BEAUTIFUL

I sit face to face with America, and I now know who I am talking with. It is America's essential self, the heart and soul beneath all that has covered her over. And it feels like the most powerful connection ever made, the kind where I am left knowing why I was born and that if I were to die tomorrow, I would have done what I came to do.

I say her words again and again: *Love does not martyr anyone. Love is what has been martyred.*

***

It is a strange place to stand, here on the bridge between the Terror of the Situation and the Hope for Our Country. I think this *is* where we stand if we can allow ourselves to know it. I, for one, want to bridge the great divide between us, and I hope you are walking with me. I see this as the next leg of our evolutionary journey, and for that, we will need a new energy source. It won't come from fossil fuels, the sun, wind, or water. It will come from inside us, from harnessing our hatred and the need to destroy and using all that energy to come back home to one another. The Hope for Our Country is that we see this now and that we can have compassion for ourselves and all others for the hard road we have often walked.

Yes, America says. *More than anything, I think we all want to belong. What we really want to belong to is love. I know that now.*

She is beautiful, this America. I can see hope and the possibility of new beginnings in her eyes. *Hope and possibility are where you came from,* I tell her, *from people who were looking for a new life in a new land.*

Yes, she answers, *but we got off to a rather bad start, didn't we? I'm a realist, too, you know. Shifting the consciousness of an entire country is perhaps next to impossible . . . and perhaps not. I am so grateful for this conversation. I won't forget the things you told me and the journey we shared here. Now, I have some work to do.*

And with that, America picked up her torch. I couldn't see if it was fully lit, but I imagine she will be back, and we will talk again.

THANK YOU

T hank you, dear reader, for taking this journey with me through the dark underbelly of human dysfunction and the seriousness of the threats we face. Thank you for continuing with me into the light of all that is possible and all that psychology today has to offer us so that we can each play a new part in ending world violence and restoring ourselves and our country to safety, peace, and love.

Please visit my website, www.phyllisleavitt.com, where you can sign in for my newsletter and the free PDF of a powerful chapter not included in this book and contact me or schedule a call about speaking on your podcast, radio show, conference, or community event. You can also find me on social media:

https://www.facebook.com/phyllis.leavitt
https://www.youtube.com/channel/UCOdxqvDK9N421AZ5TTxqUgQ
https://www.linkedin.com/in/phyllis-leavitt-630179255/
https://www.instagram.com/phyllis_e_leavitt/
https://twitter.com/PhyllisLeavitt2

ABOUT THE AUTHOR

P hyllis Leavitt, MA, graduated from Antioch University with a master's degree in psychology and counseling in 1989. She co-directed Parents United, a family-focused sexual abuse treatment program in Santa Fe, New Mexico, until 1991 and had a full-time psychotherapy practice treating children, families, couples, and individual adults for thirty-four years. She has worked extensively with abuse and dysfunctional family dynamics, their aftermath, and some of the most important elements for healing. She has published two previous books, *A Light in the Darkness* and *Into the Fire*, before completing *America in Therapy: A New Approach to Hope and Healing for a Nation in Crisis*. She lives with her husband in Taos, NM, and is retired, devoting her time to writing.

CONCLUSION

I n conclusion, here is an outline of the main points of *America in Therapy* and several suggestions for how you can help make the principles of *America in Therapy* a reality in your life.

Main Points

— The main threat to our continued survival as a nation and a species is our deteriorating mental health.

— Many of the practices and policies of our most powerful institutions mirror abuse family dynamics on the individual level and have an increasingly disastrous effect on all of us.

— Abuse dynamics are caused by and cause broken bonds of care and connection between people.

— The hope for America is to understand that conflicting ideologies are not the cause of our problem. It is our declining mental health that has us believe we are entitled to hurt others in order to get our way.

— We can best understand the roots of violence in the Family of America by looking through the lens of all we know about dysfunctional and abusive families on the individual level.

— We can make the dynamics of abuse common knowledge: blame of victims, blame of victims for their symptoms, silencing of truth-tellers, and rewards for complicity.

— Our worst symptoms are Cries for Help.

— Victim and victimizer are both victims.

— We can educate ourselves and others about High-Tech Human Relations and make them a national priority.

— We can learn and commit to the Six Elements of Repair: restraint, responsibility, reflection, rehabilitation and amends, resolution, and reconnection.

— We can embrace the urgency to rework our relationship to power and equality.

— We can understand that war is easy and that a commitment to safety, peace, and love is the hardest, most courageous, and most gratifying work we will ever do—as Americans and as humans—and that making them our number one priority could very well mean the difference between life and death for us all.

How You Can Help

— Write a review of *America in Therapy* for booksellers, newspapers, and other social media.

— Invite me to speak about *America in Therapy* on your podcast or radio show or at your conference or other community event.

— Sign up for my newsletter at www.phyllisleavitt.com and receive my free PDF of a new, not yet published chapter.

— Share this book with everyone you know.

— Share this book with people in positions of power and influence.

— Create a group for support in implementing High-Tech Human Relations and bringing them to the world around you.

— Practice High-Tech Human Relations to the best of your ability in your own life with all the people you interact with.

— Remember that the goal is not perfection; it is a commitment to get back up and try again.

— We will always have disagreement; we don't have to have war.

— Stand up to violence powerfully but without becoming violent.

— Find a safe person to do your own healing work with.

— Know that every effort you make to heal and embody High-Tech Human Relations contributes to peace, safety, and the creation of a loving and sustainable world for all of us.

ENDNOTES

1   Medina, Jennifer. "Family Ties. Political Divisions." The New York Times, November 5, 2022. https://www.nytimes.com/2022/11/05/us/politics/political-ly-divided-family.html.

2   Irsan, Nileh. "When the Thin Blue Line Breaks: Racial Divide in America." The Imprint, October 27, 2020. https://imprintnews.org/youth-voice/when-the-thin-blue-line-breaks-racial-divide-in-america/48623.

3   Gaudiano, Nicole, Joseph Zeballos-Roig, and Brent D. Griffiths. "Alexandra Ocasio-Cortez says Capitol security is not 'designed to protect women' and LGBT people after a far-right troll sexually harassed her in racist terms on the Capitol steps." Business Insider, July 14, 2022. https://www.businessinsider.com/aoc-says-us-capitol-is-not-designed-to-protect-women-lgbt-people-2022-7.

4   Tapp, Tom. "Tucker Carlson Mocks AOC's Experiences of Harassment & Misogyny Saying, 'I've Never Met Anyone Who Hates Women'." Deadline, September 8, 2022. https://deadline.com/2022/09/tucker-carlson-mocks-aoc-ocasio-cortez-1235112115/.

5   Bensinger, Ken and Sheera Frenkel. "After Mar-a-Lago Search, Talk of 'Civil War' is Flaring Online." The New York Times, October 6, 2022. https://www.nytimes.com/2022/10/05/us/politics/civil-war-social-media-trump.html.

6   Associated Press. "UN Chief: 2 Billion People Live in Conflict Areas Today." VOA News, March 31, 2022. https://www.voanews.com/a/un-chief-2-billion-people-live-in-conflict-areas-today/6509020.html.

7   United Nations Office on Drugs and Crime. "Homicide kills far more people than armed conflict, says new UNODC study." Unodc.org, July 8, 2019. https://www.unodc.org/unodc/en/press/releases/2019/Juli/homicide-kills-far-more-people-than-armed-conflict--says-new-unodc-study.html.

8   TCR Staff. "US Recidivism Rates Stay Sky High." The Crime Report, July 30, 2021. https://thecrimereport.org/2021/07/30/us-recidivism-rates-stay-sky-high/.

9   American Battlefield Trust. "Civil War Casualties: The Cost of War: Killed, Wounded, Captured, and Missing." Battlefields.org, September 15, 2012. https://www.battlefields.org/learn/articles/civil-war-casualties?ms=googlegrant&ms=googlegrant&gclid=CjwKCAjw7p6aBhBiEiwA83fGusmgUWUyFFN-ZLzzEciLij3d0WppPhr6x8yxp8wc8RnarOrWy3aUkYRoCx_4QAvD_BwE.

10 Gal, Shayanne, Madison Hall, and Taylor Ardrey. "The US had 647 mass shootings in 2022. Here's the full list." Insider, January 23, 2023. https://www.insider.com/number-of-mass-shootingsin-america-this-year-2022-5.

11 CBS News. "Read Pence's letter saying he lacks authority to decide election." Cbsnews.com, January 6, 2021. https://www.cbsnews.com/news/read-pence-letter-saying-he-lacks-authority-to-decide-election/.

12 Pilkington, Ed. "Families separated at border under Trump suffering severe trauma – study." The Guardian, November 24, 2021. https://www.theguardian.com/us-news/2021/nov/24/trump-family-separations-trauma-study.

13 Hesson, Ted. "Close to 1,000 migrant children separated by Trump yet to be reunited with parents." Reuters, February 2, 2023. https://www.reuters.com/world/us/close-1000-migrant-children-separated-by-trump-yet-be-reunited-with-parents-2023-02-02/.

14 Silva, Daniella. "'Like I am trash': Migrant children reveal stories of detention, separation." NBC News, July 29, 2018. https://www.nbcnews.com/news/latino/i-am-trash-migrant-children-reveal-stories-detention-separation-n895006.

15 ICAN. "Complicit: nuclear weapons spending increased by $1.4 billion in 2020." Icanw.org, accessed October 6, 2023.https://www.icanw.org/complicit_nuclear_weapons_spending_increased_by_1_4_billion_in_2020.

16 Cohen, Li. "Nuclear war between the U.S. and Russia would kill more than 5 billion people – just from starvation, study finds." CBS News, August 16, 2022. https://www.cbsnews.com/news/nuclear-war-5-billion-people-starvation-deaths-study/.

17 Thrush, Glenn and Matt Richtel. "A Disturbing New Pattern in Mass Shootings: Young Assailants." The New York Times, June 2, 2022. https://www.nytimes.com/2022/06/02/us/politics/mass-shootings-young-men-guns.html.

18 National Archives. "President Woodrow Wilson's 14 Points (1918)." Archives.gov, February 8, 2022. https://www.archives.gov/milestone-documents/president-woodrow-wilsons-14-points.

19   Hagan, Allison. "Braver Angels Teaches People On Opposite Ends Of The Polit-
     ical Divide To Converse Civilly." NPR Illinois, November 3, 2020. https://www.
     nprillinois.org/generationlisten/2020-11-03/teaching-people-on-opposite-
     ends-of-the-political-divide-to-converse-civilly.

20   Burnett, John. "Red/Blue Workshops try to bridge the political divide. Do they
     really work?" NPR, April 6, 2022. https://www.npr.org/2022/04/06/1090910863/
     red-blue-workshops-try-to-bridge-the-political-divide-do-they-really-work.

21   Bridges, Khiara. "POV: Stop Blaming the Poor for Their Poverty." BU Today,
     November 16, 2017. https://www.bu.edu/articles/2017/pov-blaming-victims-
     of-poverty/.

22   Kelsey, Adam. "Christine Blasey Ford, Brett Kavanaugh: Most memorable
     moments from their testimonies." ABC News, September 27, 2018. https://
     abcnews.go.com/Politics/moments-mattered-ford-kavanaugh-hearings/
     story?id=58123592.

23   Sheehey, Maeve. "Chrstine Blasey Ford lawyers call Kavanaugh investigation a
     'sham' after new details emerge." Politico, July 23, 2021. https://www.politico.
     com/news/2021/07/23/christine-blasey-ford-brett-kavanaugh-investigation-
     new-details-500652.

24   Mak, Tim. "Kavanaugh Accuser Christine Blasey Ford Continues Receiv-
     ing Threats, Lawyers Say." NPR, November 8, 2018. https://www.npr.
     org/2018/11/08/665407589/kavanaugh-accuser-christine-blasey-ford-continues-
     receiving-threats-lawyers-say.

25   Sult, Ariella. "Movements Led by Black Communities Are Too Often Met with
     Tear Gas." ACLU Indiana, June 4, 2020. https://www.aclu-in.org/en/news/
     movements-led-black-communities-are-too-often-met-tear-gas.

26   Benson, Craig. "Poverty Rate of Children Higher Than National Rate, Lower
     for Older Populations." United States Census Bureau, October 4, 2022. https://
     www.census.gov/library/stories/2022/10/poverty-rate-varies-by-age-groups.
     html#:~:text=U.S.%20Poverty%20Rate%20Is%2012.8%25%20but%20
     Varies%20Significantly%20by%20Age%20Groups.

27   Charvon, Guillaume. "Poverty Truths: Rate of Poverty in the US." ATD Fourth
     World, April 20, 2022. https://atdfourthworld-usa.org/latest-news/poverty-
     truths-rate?gclid=Cj0KCQiAsdKbBhDHARIsANJ6-jebZfOT5pdeTkxgdaFHrX
     TaWa7Z7phKZBZCuLI9Q_pJ9SPspQMZ33QaAj8vEALw_wcB.

28   Griggs, Taylor. "The Wealth Inequity Gap Is Leading to More Homelessness."
     Invisible People, January 7, 2021. https://invisiblepeople.tv/the-wealth-
     inequality-gap-is-leading-to-more-homelessness/?gclid=Cj0KCQiAsdKbBh
     DHARIsANJ6-jcWOLoWHzUnNQkmbVn4zTDKnQk_yTR1UWCTlHMQsC
     DhyXZY352vr40aAroeEALw_wcB.

29   Lazarus, David. "Wealth inequality is only getting worse." Los Angeles Times,
     October 10, 2013. https://www.latimes.com/business/la-xpm-2013-oct-10-la-fi-
     lazarus-20131011-story.html.

30 Gardner, Matthew and Steve Wamhoff. "55 Corporations Paid $0 in Federal Taxes on 2020 Profits." ITEP, April 2, 2021. https://itep.org/55-profitable-corporations-zero-corporate-tax/.

31 Murray, Mark. "Poll: 61% of Republicans still believe Biden didn't win fair and square in 2020." NBC News, September 27, 2022. https://www.nbcnews.com/meet-the-press/meetthepressblog/poll-61-republicans-still-believe-biden-didnt-win-fair-square-2020-rcna49630.

32 Carbonaro, Giulia. "40% of Americans Think 2020 Election Was Stolen, Just Days Before Midterms." Newsweek, November 2, 2022. https://www.newsweek.com/40-americans-think-2020-election-stolen-days-before-midterms-1756218.

33 Choi, Matthew. "GOP Congressman Dan Crenshaw says election deniers know they're lying." The Texas Tribune, November 4, 2022. https://www.texastribune.org/2022/11/04/dan-crenshaw-election-deniers/.

34 Werft, Meghan and Julie Ngalle. "5 Peaceful Protests That Led to Social and Political Changes." Global Citizen, July 8, 2016. https://www.globalcitizen.org/en/content/peace-protests-dallas-response/.

35 Homeboy Industries. Homeboyindustries.org, accessed October 6, 2023. https://homeboyindustries.org/?gclid=Cj0KCQjw4omaBhDqARIsADXULuU4xhNtWNi8rq0MWpQHVSQyo1CAAdhIVzLnVohqIlvqAfBeXN2X3xIaAgJcEALw_wcB.

36 Dahl, Elizabeth. "Homeboy Industries Helps Guys Get out of Gangs and Start Over." The Manual, June 9, 2017. https://www.themanual.com/culture/homeboy-industries-help-former-gang-members/.

37 LeBlanc, Paul and Annette Choi. "United States tops 400 mass shootings in 2023." CNN, July 24, 2023. https://www.cnn.com/2023/07/24/politics/us-400-mass-shootings/index.html.

38 Elflein, John. "Post-traumatic stress disorder (PTSD) – Statistics & Facts." Statista, February 11, 2021. https://www.statista.com/topics/7449/post-traumatic-stress-disorder-ptsd/#topicOverview.

39 Peterson, Jillian and James Densely. "Op-Ed: We have studied every mass shooting since 1966. Here's what we've learned about the shooters." Los Angeles Times, August 4, 2019. https://www.latimes.com/opinion/story/2019-08-04/el-paso-dayton-gilroy-mass-shooters-data?_gl=1*1et9s51*_gcl_au*MTMwMzM1Njg4LjE2OTM3NzkxNDc.

40 Haynie, Devon. "The Long-Reaching Human Toll of Sept. 11, by the Numbers." U.S. News, September 10, 2021. https://www.usnews.com/news/national-news/articles/2021-09-10/counting-the-lives-lost-as-a-result-of-9-11.

41 Peace Alliance. "Marianne Williamson." Peacealliance.org, February 28, 2018. https://peacealliance.org/team/marianne-williamson/.

42 Zhao, Christina. "Marianne Williamson Says She'll 'Harness Love' to Defeat Donald Trump in 2020 — And Twitter Had a Lot to Say." Newsweek, June 28,

2019. https://www.newsweek.com/marianne-williamson-says-shell-harness-love-defeat-donald-trump-2020-twitter-had-lot-say-1446438.

43 Branum, Guy (@guybranum). "Marianne Williamson is the only candidate bold enough to propose a witchcraft based health care system." Twitter, June 27, 2019, 6:38pm. https://twitter.com/guybranum/status/1144419886606610432?ref_src= twsrc%5Etfw%7Ctwcamp%5Etweetembed%7Ctwterm%5E1144419886606610 432%7Ctwgr%5E9085be73ce313cce7ad82c6e76cad023014e03a%7Ctwcon% 5Es1_&ref_url=https%3A%2F%2Fwww.heyalma.com%2Ftwitters-best-jokes-about-marianne-williamson%2F.

44 Williamson, Marianne (@marwilliamson). "A politics of love is not a path of passivity or weakness. It is a path of radical truth-telling, refusal to look away from unnecessary suffering, and a courageous rejection of criminal, economic and social injustice. Only big truth will have the power to defeat big lies. #mw2020." Twitter, July 25, 2019, 8:16am. https://twitter.com/marwilliamson/status/115441 0087689179136?ref_src=twsrc%5Etfw%7Ctwcamp%5Etweetembed%7Ctwterm %5E1154410087689179136%7Ctwgr%5Eb6ac18cd5c0122e37973b1041689a00 fb89e7763%7Ctwcon%5Es1_&ref_url=https%3A%2F%2Fwww.nbcnews.com %2Fthink%2Fopinion%2Fmarianne-williamson-s-democratic-debate-performance-raised-eyebrows-she-s-ncna1035956.

45 Tutu, Desmond. "Truth and Reconciliation Commission, South Africa." Britannica, September 13, 2023. https://www.britannica.com/topic/Truth-and-Reconciliation-Commission-South-Africa.

46 United States House of Representatives. "The Most Infamous Floor Brawl in the History of the U.S. House of Representatives." History.house.gov, accessed October 6, 2023. https://history.house.gov/Historical-Highlights/1851-1900/The-most-infamous-floor-brawl-in-the-history-of-the-U-S--House-of-Representatives/.

47 American Battlefield Trust. "Civil War Casualties: The Cost of War: Killed, Wounded, Captured, and Missing." Battlefields.org, September 15, 2012. https:// www.battlefields.org/learn/articles/civil-war-casualties?ms=googlegrant&ms= googlegrant&gclid=CjwKCAjw7p6aBhBiEiwA83fGusmgUWUyFFNZLzzE ciLij3d0WppPhr6x8yxp8wc8RnarOrWy3aUkYRoCx_4QAvD_BwE.

48 Reichard, Raquel. "Why Isn't Puerto Rico a State?" History.com, July 12, 2023. https://www.history.com/news/puerto-rico-statehood.

49 Bunn, Curtis. "Report: Black people are still killed by police at a higher rate than other groups." NBC News, March 3, 2022. https://www.nbcnews.com/ news/nbcblk/report-black-people-are-still-killed-police-higher-rate-groups-rcna17169.

50 Dews, Fred. "Highlights from an event on police shootings of unarmed black males in America." Brookings, October 30, 2018. https://www.brookings.edu/ articles/highlights-from-an-event-on-police-shootings-of-unarmed-black-males-in-america/.

51 Chenoweth, Erica and Maria J. Stephan. "How the world is proving Martin Luther King right about nonviolence." The Washington Post, January 18, 2016. https://www.washingtonpost.com/news/monkey-cage/wp/2016/01/18/how-the-world-is-proving-mlk-right-about-nonviolence/.

52 United Nations. "Ukraine: Over 1,500 children killed or injured, concern rises over forced transfers." News.un.org, June 1, 2023. https://news.un.org/en/story/2023/06/1137237#:~:text=More%20than%201%2C500%20killed%2C%20injured&text=Brown%20expressed%20her%20sympathy%20to,invasion%20began%2015%20months%20ago.

53 Statista Research Department. "Number of civilian casualties in Ukraine during Russia's invasion verified by OHCHR from February 24, 2022 to September 10, 2023." Statista, September 12, 2023. https://www.statista.com/statistics/1293492/ukraine-war-casualties/.

54 Roth, Andrew. "Battlefield deaths in Ukraine have risen sharply this year, say US officials." The Guardian, August 18, 2023. https://www.theguardian.com/world/2023/aug/18/ukraine-russia-war-battlefield-deaths-rise.

55 O'Sullivan, Donie. "Republican congressman posts video depicting violence against Ocasio-Cortez and Biden." CNN, November 10, 2021. https://www.cnn.com/2021/11/09/politics/gosar-anime-video-violence-ocasio-cortez-biden/index.html.

56 Gambino, Lauren. "'Inciting violence begets violence': Paul Gosar censured over video aimed at AOC." The Guardian, November 17, 2021. https://www.theguardian.com/us-news/2021/nov/17/house-censures-paul-gosar-violent-video-against-aoc.

57 Literacy Mid-South. "The Relationship Between Incarceration and Low Literacy." Literacymidsouth.org, accessed October 6, 2023. https://www.literacymidsouth.org/news/the-relationship-between-incarceration-and-low-literacy#:~:text=High%20school%20dropouts%20are%203.5,incarceration%20rate%20in%20the%20nation.

58 Wu, Cindy and Prue Brady. "Private Companies Producing with US Prison Labor in 2020: Prison Labor in the US, Part II." Corporate Accountability Lab, August 5, 2020. https://corpaccountabilitylab.org/calblog/2020/8/5/private-companies-producing-with-us-prison-labor-in-2020-prison-labor-in-the-us-part-ii.

59 Compassion Prison Project. "How Common Are Adverse Childhood Experiences (ACEs)?" compassionprisonproject.org, accessed October 6, 2023. https://compassionprisonproject.org/childhood-trauma-statistics/.

60 Rochkind, Rivka, LCPC. "Hardwired for Connection." PsychCare Psychological Services, LLC, April 14, 2016. https://www.psychcaremd.com/hardwired-for-connection/.

61 American SPCC. "Child Maltreatment Statistics." Americanspcc.org, accessed October 6, 2023. https://americanspcc.org/child-maltreatment-statistics/.

62 Mully Children's Family USA. "About Charles Mulli." Mcfus.org, accessed October 6, 2023. https://mcfus.org/about-charles-mulli/.

63 Ryan, William. Blaming the Victim. Vintage Books, a division of Random House, 1972, revised 1976.

64 Federal Bureau of Prisons. "An Inside Look at Volunteering with the BOP." Bop.gov, March 8, 2022. https://www.bop.gov/resources/news/20220308_volunteering.jsp.

65 Stevenson, Bryan. Just Mercy: A Story of Justice and Redemption. One World, an imprint of Random House. 2014.

66 AmeriCorps. "Volunteering in U.S. Hits Record High; Worth $167 Billion." Americorps.gov, November 13, 2018. https://americorps.gov/newsroom/press-releases/2018/volunteering-us-hits-record-high-worth-167-billion#:~:text=The%202018%20Volunteering%20in%20America,through%20an%20organization%20last%20year.

A free ebook edition is available with the purchase of this book.

To claim your free ebook edition:

1. Visit MorganJamesBOGO.com
2. Sign your name CLEARLY in the space
3. Complete the form and submit a photo of the entire copyright page
4. You or your friend can download the ebook to your preferred device

Morgan James
BOGO™

A **FREE** ebook edition is available for you or a friend with the purchase of this print book.

CLEARLY SIGN YOUR NAME ABOVE

Instructions to claim your free ebook edition:
1. Visit MorganJamesBOGO.com
2. Sign your name CLEARLY in the space above
3. Complete the form and submit a photo of this entire page
4. You or your friend can download the ebook to your preferred device

Print & Digital Together Forever.

Snap a photo

Free ebook

Read anywhere